The **Essential** Buyer's Guide

Ford

ESCORT

All Mk1 & Mk2 models 1967 to 1980

Your marque expert:
Dan Williamson

VELOCE PUBLISHING
THE PUBLISHER OF FINE AUTOMOTIVE BOOKS

Other books from Veloce Publishing's The **Essential** Buyer's Guide series

Alfa GT (Booker)
Alfa Romeo Spider Giulia (Booker & Talbott)
Austin Seven (Barker)
Big Healeys (Trummel)
BMW E21 3 Series (1975-1983) (Reverente, Cook)
BMW GS (Henshaw)
BSA Bantam (Henshaw)
BSA 500 & 650 Twins (Henshaw)
Citroën 2CV (Paxton)
Citroën ID & DS (Heilig)
Cobra Replicas (Ayre)
Corvette C2 Sting Ray 1963-1967 (Falconer)
Ducati Bevel Twins (Falloon)
Fiat 500 & 600 (Bobbitt)
Ford Capri (Paxton)
Harley-Davidson Big Twins (Henshaw)
Hinckley Triumph triples & fours 750, 900, 955, 1000, 1050, 1200 – 1991-2009 (Henshaw)
Honda CBR600 Hurricane (Henshaw)
Honda CBR FireBlade (Henshaw)
Honda SOHC fours 1969-1984 (Henshaw)
Jaguar E-type 3.8 & 4.2-litre (Crespin)
Jaguar E-type V12 5.3-litre (Crespin)
Jaguar XJ 1995-2003 (Crespin)
Jaguar XK8 & XKR (1996-2005) (Thorley)
Jaguar/Daimler XJ6, XJ12 & Sovereign (Crespin)
Jaguar/Daimler XJ40 (Crespin)
Jaguar Mark 1 & 2 (All models including Daimler 2.5-litre V8) 1955 to 1969 (Thorley)
Jaguar XJ-S (Crespin)
Jaguar XK 120, 140 & 150 (Thorley)
Land Rover Series I, II & IIA (Thurman)
Mazda MX-5 Miata (Mk1 1989-97 & Mk2 98-2001) (Crook)
Mercedes-Benz 280SL-560DSL Roadsters (Bass)
Mercedes-Benz 'Pagoda' 230SL, 250SL & 280SL
Roadsters & Coupés (Bass)
MGA 1955-1962 (Sear, Crosier)
MGB & MGB GT (Williams)
MG Midget & A-H Sprite (Horler)
MG TD, TF & TF1500 (Jones)
Mini (Paxton)
Morris Minor & 1000 (Newell)
New Mini (Collins)
Norton Commando (Henshaw)
Peugeot 205 GTI (Blackburn)
Porsche 911 (930) Turbo series (Streather)
Porsche 911 (964) (Streather)
Porsche 911 (993) (Streather)
Porsche 911 (996) (Streather)
Porsche 911 Carrera 3.2 series 1984 to 1989 (Streather)
Porsche 911SC – Coupé, Targa, Cabriolet & RS Model years 1978-1983 (Streather)
Porsche 924 – All models 1976 to 1988 (Hodgkins)
Porsche 928 (Hemmings)
Porsche 986 Boxster series (Streather)
Porsche 987 Boxster and Cayman series (Streather)
Rolls-Royce Silver Shadow & Bentley T-Series (Bobbitt)
Subaru Impreza (Hobbs)
Triumph Bonneville (Henshaw)
Triumph Herald & Vitesse (Davies, Mace)
Triumph Spitfire & GT6 (Baugues)
Triumph Stag (Mort & Fox)
Triumph TR6 (Williams)
Triumph TR7 & TR8 (Williams)
Vespa Scooters – Classic 2-stroke models 1960-2008 (Paxton)
VW Beetle (Cservenka & Copping)
VW Bus (Cservenka & Copping)
VW Golf GTI (Cservenka & Copping)

Animals and everything related to them!
www.hubbleandhattie.com

Books that explore any and every facet of military history
www.battlecry-books.com

www.veloce.co.uk

First published in September 2013 by Veloce Publishing Limited, Veloce House, Parkway Farm Business Park, Middle Farm Way, Poundbury, Dorchester, Dorset, DT1 3AR, England.
Fax 01305 250479/e-mail info@veloce.co.uk/web www.veloce.co.uk or www.velocebooks.com.
ISBN: 978-1-845845-25-4 UPC: 6-36847-04525-8
Readers with ideas for automotive books, or books on other transport or related hobby subjects, are invited to write to the editorial director of Veloce Publishing at the above address.
British Library Cataloguing in Publication Data – A catalogue record for this book is available from the British Library.
Typesetting, design and page make-up all by Veloce Publishing Ltd on Apple Mac. Printed in India by Replika Press.

Introduction
– the purpose of this book

Choose your weapon – the Mk1 Escort (left) gave way to the Mk2 shape (right) at the start of 1975.

Ford's Mk1 and Mk2 Escorts achieved legendary status through their amazing success – on roads, rally stages and racetracks. Millions were sold around the world, with Escorts proving to be winners in the hands of the car-buying public and motorsport champions alike.

Today, old Escorts have become collectable classics, providing a massively diverse choice of models that's unmatched by virtually any other car. From affordable little runabouts to bank-breaking, fire-breathing rally monsters, Escorts are truly capable of everything.

Introduced at the end of 1967 as an all-new, small family saloon to replace the ageing Anglia, the Escort Mk1 combined a range of fresh engines, transmissions and running gear into a thoroughly conventional package. Under the bonnet was a simple Kent Crossflow powerplant in 1100cc or 1300cc guise, coupled to a delightful four-speed manual or three-speed automatic gearbox and finely-balanced rear-wheel drive chassis. It incorporated MacPherson strut front suspension, live rear axle, rack-and-pinion steering, and the option of disc front brakes.

It wasn't revolutionary or especially innovative, but the Escort was good at everything – and, in some cases, exceptionally good.

While the basic Escort was praised for the roominess of its small, stylish body, motorsport teams took advantage of its low weight, high strength and foolproof handling. Before long, the Escort 1300GT was cross-bred with Lotus Cortina mechanicals to create the Escort Twin Cam. And in no time at all, the Ford Escort had redefined rallying, circuit racing and the whole concept of sporting cars.

Further high-performance Escorts quickly followed, including the RS1600, Mexico and RS2000 built by Advanced Vehicle Operations (AVO) in Aveley, Essex.

All the while, mainstream models were gradually improving; offering a huge choice of two-door and four-door saloons, along with load-lugging vans and practical estates. Trim levels ranged from pure poverty to real luxury, culminating in the plush 1300E, complete with real-wood dashboard cappings.

Production of the Mk1 – in Britain, Germany and numerous other countries around the globe – stopped at the end of 1974, when it was replaced by the Escort Mk2. Again offered in a variety of body styles, the new model looked outwardly quite different; now featuring a heavier, squared-off shape with larger glass area. But much of the new car's underpinnings – right down to the floorpan – were exactly the same as its predecessor's.

Now, though, there was a 1600cc engine available in run-of-the-mill models, including the cheerful Sport and opulent Ghia. Naturally, high-performance Escorts stepped up a notch, including the hardcore, limited-run RS1800, UK-only RS Mexico, and stunning RS2000, which boasted an aerodynamic droop-snoot nose.

By then the Escort had become a firm favourite among practical motorists, enthusiastic drivers, and international rally champions – a feeling that continued long after the Mk2 stopped production in July 1980.

In spite of that, the Escort's cheap, humble origins and huge numbers meant many were abused, neglected, and allowed to rust away. Which makes finding a nice example today a task that's tinged with the danger of bodged-together wrecks, fake RSs and overly-inflated prices.

This book aims to help you buy an Escort that's as good to drive as it is to look at. Whether it's to restore, modify, or simply use as a reliable everyday classic, we hope you're rewarded with an Escort that's exactly right for you.

Sporting Escorts achieved legendary status through rallying, giving rise to terrific road cars, including the Mk2 RS Mexico.

Thanks

Big thanks to everyone who's helped along the way, especially Richard Moore but also Richard Farrell, Jason Taylor, Steve Ogle, Dave Robinson, and Sarah Mortimer.

Contents

The Essential Buyer's Guide™ currency
At the time of publication a BG unit of currency "●" equals approximately £1.00 (US$1.57/Euro 1.17). Please adjust to suit current exchange rates using sterling as the base currency.

1 Is it the right car for you?
– marriage guidance

**Snug by modern standards, but a great driving position, even for tall drivers.
This is a Mk1 cabin in four-door form.**

Tall and short drivers
Plenty of headroom and seat adjustment, even for very tall drivers.

Weight of controls
Escorts are loved for their precise controls – a slick gear change, responsive steering, sharp handling and instant throttle (especially on sporting variants). There's no power-assisted steering, though, and modified cars often use a stiff motorsport clutch.

Will it fit in the garage?
Length: 156.6in (3978mm) to 163.1in (4142mm)
Width: 60.5in (1537mm) to 62.8in (1595mm)
Height: 53.0in (1346mm) to 55.5in (1410mm)

Interior space
Roomy in their day, but pretty cramped by modern standards. Fine for carrying four adults, although bulky RS seats reduce rear legroom.

Luggage capacity
Good, usable load space in all but the Twin Cam, RS1600 and early Mexico, which

had a battery in the boot and spare wheel engulfing the floor. Estates are very practical even today.
Saloon: 10.3cu ft (292 litres)
Estate: 31.53cu ft (893 litres)

Running costs
With lightweight bodies and relatively small engines, Escorts are remarkably frugal – only twin-carb RSs drink the juice. Servicing is cheap and simple on everything but twin-camshaft engines. Most repairs are easy, if not quite as inexpensive as you'd expect for a little old Ford.

Unless it's an AVO Mk1 with floor-mounted spare wheel, there's plenty of luggage space in an old Escort – here in Mk2 Ghia guise.

Usability
Ideal family cars when new, Escorts are reliable, practical and still used on a daily basis by dedicated drivers. Just make sure you're security-conscious.

Parts availability
Almost everything is available new or secondhand (including a world of modified parts), although trim (especially interior) can be difficult or virtually impossible to track down.

Parts cost
Mechanical components can come in at cheap-and-cheerful small-Ford prices, rising to supercar levels for specialist BDA engine parts. Body and trim costs follow a similar pattern – inexpensive for readily-available spares, but bearing a massive Rallye Sport premium for anything rare and/or desirable.

Insurance
Limited-mileage and classic car insurance is available for any model, meaning reasonable costs. Even ultra-rare and highly-modified Escorts shouldn't be overly expensive to cover.

Investment potential
Cash in an old Escort is safer than money in the bank, but prices at the upper end have probably plateaued.

Alternatives
Ford Capri, Ford Cortina Mk1/Mk2, Opel Manta, Vauxhall Chevette, Vauxhall Firenza, Triumph Dolomite, BMW 1602/2002/E21.

2 Cost considerations
– affordable, or a money pit?

Purchase price

Do you buy an Escort with your heart or your head? If it's the latter, you're in a minority. Take time to stop and think before splashing out on that 'barn-find' restoration project – you could easily spend more rebuilding a wreck (especially if you hire someone else to do the work) than you'd pay for an excellent condition Escort outright.

If your budget is tight, it may be worth investing in a tatty but roadworthy example. Then you can enjoy Escort ownership while repairing when funds allow.

Parts prices fall into two distinct categories: the cheap, basic components shared by all variations of a popular family car; and the rare, expensive spares sought-after by concours-condition RS owners. There's very little middle ground.

RS badge on any Escort part adds a price premium – as these wide steel wheels will testify.

Mechanical components like this 1300cc Crossflow engine can be cheap and easy to replace.

Parts prices (new, non-genuine unless stated)

Steering rack (exchange) ●x35
Brake discs (pair) ●x23.50
Brake pads ●x7.50
Wheel bearing ●x18.95
Track rod end ●x11.75
Front coil spring ●x20
Crossflow clutch kit ●x50
Mk2 battery tray ●x25
Mk1 front wing ●x190
Mk2 front wing ●x85
Mk2 rear light ●x30
Mk1 indicators (genuine) ●x195 pair
Mk1 front panel ●x75
Mk2 front panel ●x93
Mk1 slam panel ●x52
H4 headlamp ●x32
Mk2 grille ●x140
Outer sill ●x32
Floor repair section, front ●x46
Floor repair section, rear ●x53
Laminated windscreen ●x80
Front windscreen rubber ●x32
Carpet set ●x140

RS2000 centre console ●x150
Headlining ●x102
Seat retrim ●x650

Parts prices (secondhand – prices can vary enormously depending on condition)

Pinto 2.0 engine ●x100
Crossflow 1.6 engine ●x200
Crossflow gearbox ●x35
Mk1 grille ●x60
Mk2 grille ●x80
Mk2 bonnet ●x60
Mk1 door ●x100
Twin Cam steel wheels (set) ●x350
Mk2 Mexico steel wheels (set) ●x150
Mk1 cloth back seat ●x75

3 Living with an Escort
– will you get along together?

You don't need to be an Escort obsessive to enjoy life with a Mk1 or Mk2 – but you'll soon turn into one.

Rear-wheel-drive Escorts have a quick ability to get under your skin, and it's fair to say most current owners have kept at least one example in their fleet for decades.

Similarly, countless competition drivers, motorsport workshops and performance car collections around the world have a sporting Escort kicking around – sometimes still for serious rallying, but often purely for fun. Escorts are simply addictive.

Needless to say, prices of particularly sought-after models (such as the ultra-rare RS1800, Twin Cam and RS1600) are beyond the reach of most pockets, and values of Escorts with famous motorsport careers are stratospheric.

But don't let that put you off, because the Escort range really does offer something for everyone.

Despite the old age of Mk1s and Mk2s, most models are still perfectly capable of performing the everyday duties of a practical family car – especially in four-door form. Their cabins are a little cramped compared to modern hatchbacks, yet any (unmodified) Escort should seat four adults in relative comfort. Don't expect electric windows, air conditioning, or even reclining seats on some models. Yet don't be surprised to find an immediately inviting driving position and remarkably good ride quality (in a properly-maintained, unmodified machine).

Front seat belts were fitted to most Mk1s and virtually all Mk2s, with rears always optional in the latter. Static belts were common on early cars, but by now most have been retrofitted with inertia-reels.

On the subject of safety, old Escorts obviously don't feature airbags, anti-lock braking systems, side-impact protection or advanced crumple zones. But a good, rot-free Escort bodyshell is strong for its size – just ask all the rally drivers who regularly go bouncing off into the scenery in their machines …

All Escorts have impressive boot space; estate models in particular (made from 1968 until 1980) provide cavernous capacity with the back seat folded flat. They're cheap to buy, too.

The vast majority of Mk1s and Mk2s came equipped with 1100cc or 1300cc Kent Crossflow engines, which were tough, reliable and remarkably economical. In Weber carburettor-fed GT guise they were relatively good performers, revving happily around the clock.

Service intervals are, of course, more regular than for 21st century vehicles, but most of the parts cost pennies and the work can be tackled

The early RS1600 would be wonderful to own, drive and display – albeit expensive to buy or restore.

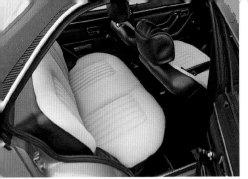

A practical family car in four-door form, and pretty luxurious in Mk2 Ghia trim, too.

Escort estate bodywork was mostly the same on Mk1 and Mk2; all had cavernous load capacity.

by home mechanics. Indeed, DIY maintenance was almost a prerequisite of Escort ownership, requiring little more than a basic toolkit – a key point that's still true today, unless you're intending to tackle a full-on restoration. Even then, your biggest worries will revolve around rust (lots and lots of rust) and sourcing hard-to-find panels and trim. The oily bits are generally easy.

The Escort's stock four-speed manual gearbox (automatic transmission was an optional extra) has one of the slickest shifts known to man, coupled to a lightweight clutch pedal; only the parts' relative weakness when used hard is a real letdown. Still, a gearbox swap is only an hour's job.

Similarly, Escort running gear is straightforward to work on, cheap to replace, and tough enough to withstand many miles. With MacPherson struts up front and leaf springs at the back, it's not only a conventional, old-fashioned setup, but arguably also the Escort's crowning glory – the success and desirability of rear-wheel-drive Escorts is arguably down to their foolproof handling, easily allowing understeer or tail-slides depending on suspension settings.

Early cars wore drum brakes all round, but bigger-engined models and most surviving Escorts have servo-assisted discs on the front – a very wise decision, and an almost essential upgrade for an everyday Escort today.

In fact, an endless scope for modifications is in many respects what Mk1s and Mk2s are all about. Okay, they're not the fastest cars in a straight line (although customised cars can be scarily quick), but they're always fun. Besides, Ford offered factory-modified Escorts from new, plus a huge range of Rallye Sport parts for use in motorsport or simply to improve road cars.

RS Escorts (we include Twin Cams and Mk1 Mexicos in the term, even though they lack the badge) were supplied new with strengthened components and enlarged engines, most of which are equally easy to maintain – only the twin-camshaft powerplants require specialist advice.

The only problem is the 'scene tax' applied to such sporting Fords, which inflates the price of anything with an RS badge – whether you're talking complete cars or the smallest of parts.

Thanks to their great looks, strong heritage, current cool factor and minimal security, sporting Escorts are also something of a high theft risk, so don't expect to leave an RS in a dim-lit city-centre car park at night.

Still, any Mk1 or Mk2 makes a fine choice for almost every occasion. Whether it's for track days, weekend drives, competitive motorsport or polishing at a show, an Escort will be the perfect companion.

4 Relative values
– which model for you?

There's an Escort for every taste and almost any occasion – but not necessarily every budget …

Thanks to immense rallying success, sporting Escorts are in greatest demand, usually referred to as RS (Rallye Sport) or AVO (Advanced Vehicle Operations) machines, the latter relating only to Mk1s.

Values of Escorts are linked to rarity, heritage and ability. Most expensive and sought-after are the exciting yet complicated twin-camshaft engined Escorts (RS1600, RS1800 and, of course, Twin Cam), with which Ford gained innumerable motorsport victories. Their more-accessible siblings (Mexico, RS Mexico and RS2000) were almost identical but for conventional powerplants, and were built in vastly greater numbers.

It goes almost without saying that AVO/RS Escorts are considerably more costly than their run-of-the-mill counterparts – in some cases worth 20 times as much.

Mainstream Escorts were made in the millions, with Mk1s running from 1967 to 1974, and Mk2s taking over until 1980. The GT and Sport are the most desirable of ordinary Escorts, followed by the luxurious 1300E (Mk1) and Ghia (Mk2).

Bear in mind, though, that any basic two-door bodyshell is worth roughly double that of a four-door. Due to their rarity, vans tend to fetch a little more than four-door Escorts, while in today's market estates are least valuable of all.

All Mk1s and Mk2s are essentially similar underneath, so if you simply want a rear-wheel-drive Escort to use, restore and maybe modify (rather than as a showpiece or investment), any model could be worth a look.

Values – a rough guide based on equality of condition

Standard four-door – 10%
Standard two-door – 20%
GT/Sport/1300E (two-door) – 45%
Harrier (Sport-based limited edition) – 55%
Mexico – 90%
RS2000/RS Mexico – 100%
Twin Cam – 200%
RS1600 – 200%
RS1800 – 225%

RS1800s are the ultimate Mk2 Escorts, but with only 109 built are now extremely sought-after and subject to fakery.

Escorts needn't be expensive – the four-door Mk1 bodystyle fetches less than half the price of its fewer-doored stablemates.

5 Before you view
– be well informed

To avoid a wasted journey, and the disappointment of finding that the car does not match your expectations, it will help if you're very clear about what questions you want to ask before you pick up the telephone. Some of these points might appear basic, but when you're excited about the prospect of buying your dream Escort, it's amazing how some of the most obvious things slip the mind ... Also check car magazines and websites for the current values of the model you are interested in, which give price guides and auction results.

Where is the car?
Is it going to be worth travelling to the next county/state, or even across a border? A locally advertised car, although it may not sound very interesting, can add to your knowledge for very little effort, so make a visit – it might even be in better condition than expected.

Dealer or private sale?
Establish early on if the car is being sold by its owner or by a trader. A private owner should have all the history, so don't be afraid to ask detailed questions. A dealer may have more limited knowledge of a car's history, but should have some documentation. A dealer may offer a warranty/guarantee (ask for a printed copy) and more of a comeback if that pricey RS turns out to be a fake.

Cost of collection and delivery
A dealer may well be used to quoting for delivery by car transporter. A private owner may agree to meet you halfway, but only agree to this after you have seen the car at the vendor's address to validate the documents. Conversely, you could meet halfway and agree the sale, but insist on meeting at the vendor's address for the handover.

View – when and where?
It is always preferable to view at the vendor's home or business premises. In the case of a private sale, the car's documentation should tally with the vendor's name and address. Arrange to view only in daylight and avoid a wet day; most cars look better in poor light or when wet.

Reason for sale?
Do make it one of the first questions. Why is the car being sold and how long has it been with the current owner? How many previous owners? Bear in mind many Escorts have really been around the block, so don't judge too harshly.

Left-hand drive to right-hand drive
With a shortage of good, rust-free Mk1s and Mk2s, it's not unusual for two-door Escorts to be imported from warmer countries. Some of these cars are left-hand drive, and may even have different trim for foreign markets. Other than a handful of Sports and RSs, most imported Escorts are sourced purely for their bodyshells, and subsequently rebuilt to the owner's preferred specification. When viewing a left-

hand drive car, remember the cost of a steering conversion is a fraction the price of welding and repanelling a rotten body.

Condition (body/chassis/interior/mechanicals)

Ask for an honest appraisal of the car's condition. Ask specifically about some of the check items described in chapter 7.

All original specification?

An original-equipment car is invariably of higher value than a customised version. But Escorts with period factory accessories may command a premium, as can the more commonplace models with well-executed mechanical modifications. Approved adaptations for historic motorsport make some special Escorts very valuable indeed.

Matching data/legal ownership

Do VIN/chassis, engine numbers and licence plate match the official registration document? Is the owner's name and address recorded in the official registration documents?

For those countries that require an annual test of roadworthiness, does the car have a document showing it complies (an MoT certificate in the UK, which can be verified on 0845 600 5977)?

If required, does the car carry a current road fund licence/license plate tag?

Does the vendor own the car outright? Money might be owed to a finance company or bank: the car could even be stolen. Several organisations will supply the data on ownership, based on the car's licence plate number, for a fee. Such companies can often also tell you whether the car has been 'written off' by an insurance company. In the UK these organisations can supply vehicle data:

HPI – 01722 422 422
AA – 0870 600 0836
DVLA – 0870 240 0010
RAC – 0870 533 3660

Other countries will have similar organisations.

Unleaded fuel

If desired, has the car been modified to run on unleaded fuel? Kent and Pinto engines will tolerate unleaded if a lead additive is used, but unleaded valve seats are a bonus – especially on a pricey BDA or Twin Cam.

Insurance

Check with your existing insurer before setting out; your current policy might not cover you to drive the car if you do purchase it.

How you can pay?

A cheque/check will take several days to clear and the vendor may prefer to sell to a cash buyer. However, a banker's draft (a cheque issued by a bank) is as good as cash, but safer, so contact your own bank and become familiar with the formalities that are necessary to obtain one.

Buying at auction?

If the intention is to buy at auction see chapter 10 for further advice.

Professional vehicle check (mechanical examination)

There are often marque/model specialists who will undertake professional examination of a vehicle on your behalf. Owners' clubs will be able to put you in touch with such specialists.

Other organisations that will carry out a general professional check in the UK are:

AA – 0800 085 3007 (motoring organisation with vehicle inspectors)

ABS – 0800 358 5855 (specialist vehicle inspection company)

RAC – 0870 533 3660 (motoring organisation with vehicle inspectors)

Other countries will have similar organisations.

6 Inspection equipment
– these items will really help

This book
Reading glasses (if you need them for close work)
Magnet (not powerful; a fridge magnet is ideal)
Torch
Probe (a small screwdriver works very well)
Overalls
Mirror on a stick
Digital camera
A friend, preferably a knowledgeable enthusiast

Before you rush out of the door, gather together a few items that will help as you work your way around the car. This book is designed to be your guide at every step, so take it along and use the check boxes to help you assess each area of the car you're interested in. Don't be afraid to let the seller see you using it.

Take your reading glasses if you need them to read documents and make close-up inspections.

A magnet will help you check if the car is full of filler, or has fibreglass panels. Use the magnet to sample bodywork areas all around the car, but be careful not to damage the paintwork. Expect to find a little filler here and there, but not whole panels. There's nothing wrong with fibreglass panels, but a purist might want the car to be as original as possible.

A torch with fresh batteries will be useful for peering into the wheelarches and under the car.

A small screwdriver can be used – with care – as a probe, particularly in the wheelarches and on the underside. With this you should be able to check an area of severe corrosion, but be cautious – if it's really bad the screwdriver might go right through the metal!

Be prepared to get dirty. Take along a pair of overalls, if you have them. Fixing a mirror at an angle on the end of a stick may seem odd, but you'll probably need it to check the condition of the underside of the car. It will also help you to peer into some of the important crevices. You can also use it, together with the torch, along the underside of the sills and on the floor.

If you have the use of a digital camera, take it along so that later you can study some areas of the car more closely. Take a picture of any part of the car that causes you concern, and seek a friend's opinion.

Ideally, have a friend or knowledgeable enthusiast accompany you: a second opinion is always valuable – especially if the car you're viewing is a pricey RS.

7 Fifteen minute evaluation
– walk away or stay?

General condition
First impressions count. An Escort that's been neglected, abused or is somehow trying to trick you may be obvious from ten paces. So how does it sit? Is the ride height what you'd expect? How fresh is the paint? Does the bodyshell look correct for the year and model? Has it been modified? Has it been hacked around and butchered? Is it pretending to be something it's not? In short, does it look right?

Escorts – in particular the valuable sporting models – have always been a target for crooks and bodgers, so it's sometimes best to presume there's a hidden problem that it's your job to spot.

Seek the opinion of an expert if necessary, and make sure you've researched the model before viewing. Don't be distracted by falling in love with the first car you see.

First impressions count. If an Escort looks straight, chances are it's worth a second glance.

Examine the bodywork and ride height to see if it looks level. Bear in mind Escort panel gaps weren't perfect even when new.

Body and chassis
Look for rust, filler, or evidence of bad welding ... everywhere! An Escort's shadow would rot if it could!

Imagine your prospective purchase has been dragged out of a swamp before being stuck back together and treated to a fresh coat of paint. Inspect every panel for ripples or blisters, make use of your magnet to check for corrosion, take a torch and poke around underneath, lift the carpets and peer into every corner, ever mindful of corrosion, cracks, creases or signs of accident damage.

Rot is probably the biggest Escort killer. This is the remains of a Mk2's sill.

The front wings, door posts, roof pillars, sills, floorpans, chassis rails, wheelarches, door frames, boot floor and suspension mounts are prime spots for serious rot. All are potential places you'll find corrosion, poor repairs, body filler or heavily-disguising underseal.

Take your time and double-check any area you're not sure about. You can't be too careful …

Underbonnet

If an Escort's inner wings look straight and sound, almost anything else can be forgiven!

What you don't want to see is corrosion or filler, notably on the slam panel, along the bulkhead and its seams, around the suspension tops (and underneath, viewed from within the wheelarches), across the drip rails or beneath the radiator.

Similarly, evidence of chopped-up panelwork (possibly due to poor repairs or fitting of an unusual engine) is a warning sign.

Of course, now is your chance to cast your eye over the engine, looking for leaks, symptoms of head gasket failure or bodged-up modifications.

The underbonnet area is also where you might find several indications of fakery (see below) …

An Escort's heart is its engine bay, revealing the condition of bodywork and mechanicals. In this case it's a Pinto-powered RS Mexico.

Test drive

At this stage, a brief test drive should be enough to tell you whether an Escort is mechanically sound.

Ask the owner to start the car from cold while you watch the exhaust for smoke and listen for any knocking or rattling from the engine. Ensure it idles without stalling and, as the engine warms up, be aware of on any noises – ticking tappets or mild piston slap should soon disappear.

A brief road test should be enough to check an Escort is mechanically sound.

If you're fully insured, take the car for a drive. Even a small-engined Escort should feel eager, if a little harsh. It should rev easily and pull in any gear. And, unless it's been modified with a race gearbox, paddle clutch and ultra-stiff suspension, everything about the car will feel user-friendly and simple to control.

If you notice poor performance, a misfire, difficulty engaging gears, clutch slip or any unusual noises or vibrations, start asking questions. Remember, though, most Escorts are mechanically cheap and simple, and drivetrain issues are generally less of a worry than bodywork problems.

Talking of which, pay particular attention to whether an Escort drives in a straight line, has positive steering and precise handling. If not, start investigating – it could be due to worn running gear, but may also be evidence of accident damage, bad repairs or serious rot.

Interior

The condition of an Escort's cabin often indicates how well it's been looked after. Torn or inappropriate seats, a fascia chopped out for extra switches, a ripped carpet, holes in the door cards or missing centre console can cost a fortune to put right – especially if you're thinking about buying a show car.

If it's a sporting Mk1 or a Mk2 RS2000, check the dashboard to make sure it's a factory pressing rather than DIY-altered. Remember that virtually all RS models until 1978 had a black headlining rather than putty-coloured.

A clean, unmolested cabin can save thousands if you're planning a restoration.

Be sure to lift the carpets and kick panels where possible because floorpan rot can be extensive and expensive to fix. Make sure the front seats aren't rattling around on their runners.

Have a look in the luggage compartment, too, checking for rot in the spare wheel well, under the fuel tank and all around the boot floor – if it's immaculate here, it often points to a good bodyshell. The boot is also a prime place for determining the age of an Escort and whether it's equipped with the proper AVO or RS additions.

Modifications

If you're planning on owning a heavily-modified Escort, buying a pre-converted car could work out cheaper than doing the conversion yourself. Ford offered vast amounts of uprated parts and accessories from new, so they're certainly not to be frowned upon.

Bear in mind that although some Escorts are treated to craftsman-like workmanship, others have a big engine thrown in and the bodywork hacked around to make it fit.

Tasteful engine transplants (such as Cosworth or Duratec swaps) can work wonderfully and add value, but make sure the car's suspension, brakes and transmission have been upgraded to cope with the added power. Standard Escort bodyshells can split under hard use, so check for stress fractures around the seams. Don't be surprised to see a roll cage or stitch welds for strength.

Be wary of DIY efforts to make non-standard parts fit. Some owners skimp on costs (say, welding a sump rather than buying an off-the-shelf alloy item). Such parts may be adequate, but don't be fooled into paying over the odds – and be extra vigilant for hidden bodges elsewhere.

Modifications can increase an Escort's value – especially tasteful parts like genuine RS alloy wheels.

Try to steer clear of any Escort with customised bodywork. Rallye Sport spoilers, authentic-looking wide wheelarches and non-standard paintwork are just about the only exterior alterations that won't adversely affect the asking price. Other than wheels, of course – genuine RS alloys or wide steels (depending on the car) can be a bonus.

Oh, and don't forget that a heavily-modified car can be a bind to use on anything but track days or clear, empty roads. Highly-tuned Escorts are heavy on fuel, noisy, uncomfortable, difficult to insure, intolerant of traffic, awkward to start from cold, have heavy controls and need constant servicing. They're also immense fun and incredibly rewarding to drive fast …

Identity

Avoiding fakes and ringers is crucial when buying an old Escort, especially if it's claiming to be a rare RS. Not that there's anything wrong with a nice replica or reshelled car – unless it's priced like the real thing.

Sadly, it's not unusual to see a mocked-up Mexico or RS2000 wearing the wrong identity – so be on your guard.

Escorts originally had a vehicle number stamped into the offside inner wing around the strut top, but most have now been replaced. A matching number was stamped into the chassis plate – until August 1970 and from January 1980 (November 1979 in Germany) the plate was mounted on the offside inner wing, while between those dates it was found on the slam panel. Plates were riveted into place, but are available new and easily swapped between cars – so beware...

Deciphering the vehicle number lets you work out the car's build date and place of assembly. Meanwhile, codes on the chassis plate relate to the model, engine, colour and so on.

Check the chassis plate to ensure it matches the car's alleged identity.

Vehicle number
Country of origin
B = Ford Great Britain
C = Ford Great Britain (affiliated assembly)
E = Ford Germany (affiliated assembly)
G = Ford Germany

Assembly plant
B = Halewood
C = Saarlouis
F = Aveley
J = Boreham
K = Sydney

Body type
Pre-August 1970
40 = Standard two-door
41 = Super estate
42 = De Luxe two-door
43 = De Luxe estate
44 = Super two-door
48 = GT two-door
49 = Twin Cam or RS1600 two-door
50 = Standard van (6cwt)
51 = De Luxe van (8cwt)
5A = Standard van (8cwt)
5D = De Luxe four-door
5G = GT four-door
5P = Super four-door

BBATMK42002

BBATMK42002

BBATMK42002

5S = Standard four-door
AT = Export two-door
AF = Export four-door
AD = Export estate
AV = Van

Post-August 1970
AT = Escort two-door
AF = Escort four-door
AD = Escort estate
AV = Escort van

Year and month of production

BBATMK42002

Year code	Year built	Jan	Feb	Mar	Apr	May	June	July	Aug	Sep	Oct	Nov	Dec
G	1967	C	K	D	E	L	Y	S	T	J	U	M	P
H	1968	B	R	A	G	C	K	D	E	L	Y	S	T
J	1969	J	U	M	P	B	R	A	G	C	K	D	E
K	1970	L	Y	S	T	J	U	M	P	B	R	A	G
L	1971	C	K	D	E	L	Y	S	T	J	U	M	P
M	**1972**	B	R	A	G	C	**K**	D	E	L	Y	S	T
N	1973	J	U	M	P	B	R	A	G	C	K	D	E
P	1974	L	Y	S	T	J	U	M	P	B	R	A	G
R	1975	C	K	D	E	L	Y	S	T	J	U	M	P
S	1976	B	R	A	G	C	K	D	E	L	Y	S	T
T	1977	J	U	M	P	B	R	A	G	C	K	D	E
U	1978	L	Y	S	T	J	U	M	P	B	R	A	G
W	1979	C	K	D	E	L	Y	S	T	J	U	M	P
A	1980	B	R	A	G	C	K	D	E	L	Y	S	T

Serial number

The car's unique serial number, counted in order of vehicles produced during the month.

BBATMK42002

BBATMK42002

Drive

Pre-August 1970

1 = right-hand drive
2 = left-hand drive

Drive	Engine	Trans	Axle	Colour	Trim
2	J3	5	X	H5	K1
					BS. AU

Post-August 1970

1 or A = left-hand drive
2 or B = right-hand drive

Engine (where used)

C or G1 = 1098cc low compression
B or G2 = 1098cc high compression
T or J1 = 1298cc low compression
S or J2 = 1298cc high compression
R or J3 = 1298cc GT
L3 or L7 = 1598cc GT
Z or K6 = 1558cc (Twin Cam)
V, K5 or L5= 1601cc (RS1600)
LE = 1593cc (RS Mexico)
NE = 1998cc (RS2000)

Drive	Engine	Trans	Axle	Colour	Trim
2	J3	5	X	H5	K1
					BS. AU

Trans

1, 5 or B = manual   7 or D = automatic

Drive	Engine	Trans	Axle	Colour	Trim
2	J3	5	X	H5	K1
					BS. AU

Version (where used)
A = RS2000
B = RS Mexico
C = Sport/RS2000
D = base/L
E = Ghia
G = GT or Mexico
L = Twin Cam, RS1600 or RS2000
M = L
P = XL/GL
Q = Sport/RS2000
S = base/standard
W = 1300E
Z = GXL

FORD MOTOR CO. LTD.
LONDON, ENGLAND

Type	Version	Vehicle No	
ATH	P	BBATMK42002	

You can usually identify an Escort's body by what was spot-welded at the factory – here we see a Mk2 RS's spare wheel strap bracket in the boot.

Bodyshell identity

Escorts are somewhat prone to having their identities swapped around, so it's wise to check a car's body matches its age:

• External bonnet release, small hinge supports, and prop laid across slam panel until summer 1969.

• Pre-September 1969 fuel tank had a long neck and protruding cap.

• Mk1 door locks were separate from handles after summer 1969.

• Bonnet-mounted windscreen washer nozzle until 1970, with notched ends on the bulkhead heater dome.

• Mk1 had a factory-welded bulkhead bracket for the washer reservoir from late 1969 (not AVO models). The earlier setup featured a three-pin mount for a cheese-wedge-shaped bottle.

• The Mk1 dashboard had large switch holes until September 1970.

• Slanting rear shock absorbers until upright mounts in November 1973.

• Strut tops – large (105mm) before February 1977, small (85mm) thereafter.

• Mk2 bulkhead – five dimples before February 1977, seven thereafter.

• Mk2 slam panel – rounded edges before February 1977, square thereafter.

Type 49 bodyshell (Mk1)

If you're looking at a Mk1 Twin Cam, RS1600, Mexico or RS2000, you'll need to check it has the proper bodyshell, known as a Type 49 (due to early model designations). All the above Mk1s had these specially strengthened bodies, with many hand-made modifications (so don't be alarmed if the cutting and welding looks rough). Despite what some sellers might say, there were no exceptions!

Type 49s wore the following:
- Front wings with flared wheelarches (also on Sport and 1300E).
- Heavy-duty inner wings with reinforced strut top plates and towers (visible from under the wheelarchs).
- Uprated rear spring mounts with boxed-in sections.
- Rear radius rod brackets welded to the chassis rails.
- Rolled rear wheelarches.
- Six-dial dashboard pressing (also on GT, post-August 1972 Sport, late-spec XL and 1300E).
- Reworked transmission tunnel with the gearstick hole closer to the handbrake than standard, plus rough trimming of the tunnel strengthener and bashing of the metalwork to make the 'box fit.
- Eight bolts through the boot floor for a stone guard (which may be missing or not fitted from standard). Some early Sports also had these bolts.
- Different exhaust hangers from standard.
- Spare wheel hook on the boot floor (not RS2000 or post-October 1972 Mexico).
- Vehicle number starting BB49 (Twin Cam/early RS1600) or BFAT. Earliest few Twin Cams and GTs started in BB48.
- Battery tray in spare wheel well (not RS2000 or post-October 1972 Mexico).
- Dressed-back bulkhead lip on RS1600s and some early Mexicos.

Mk2 RS bodyshell

All Mk2 RS bodies were built in Germany (except Aussie RS2000s, and 1975 RS1800s based on British 1600 Sports). All German RSs featured neat, factory-fitted shell strengthening and modifications – so walk away if a car claiming to be an RS lacks any of the following:
- Heavy-duty inner wings with reinforced strut top plates and towers (visible from under the wheelarchs).
- Uprated rear spring mounts with boxed-in sections.
- Rear radius rod brackets welded to the chassis rails.
- Reworked transmission tunnel with neatly-pressed gearstick aperture factory-welded closer to the handbrake than standard, chopped-out strengthener and slight bashing around the bulkhead.
- Different exhaust hangers from standard.
- Spare wheel strap hook on the boot floor next to the wheel well (also on Escort Harrier).
- Speedometer cable bracket on offside floorpan.
- Unique radiator housing with cutout upper section and revised lower crossmember.
- Fuel line clips on nearside chassis rail.
- Washer bottle on offside inner wing (RS2000 and RS Mexico).
- Vehicle number starting GCAT.

8 Key points
– where to look for problems

Spot the rot
Escorts rot. A lot. You'll be lucky to find an Escort that's not showing signs of corrosion.

Check everywhere for rust, splits or filler. Start at the front panel, move to the bonnet, front wings, inner and outer sills, door posts, door frames, roof pillars, rear wings, back panel and boot lid.

Underneath, examine the suspension mounting points, the entire chassis rails, lower bulkhead, floorpans, spare wheel well and boot floor.

Beware rust! This used to be a Mk2 door frame ...

Underbonnet
Make sure it's the right engine with the right parts for the model. Check an RS or AVO car has the proper reinforcing plates, battery position, bulkhead and radiator position.

Again, look everywhere for signs of rot. Inspect the strut tops, suspension towers, slam panel, bulkhead, chassis legs and drip rails.

The right engine in the right car – here, an RS1800's BDA sits between the proper RS inner wings.

Beware of fakes

AVO/RS Escorts are desirable, valuable and regularly replicated. If you're paying serious cash for a car, you need to avoid anything dodgy. Research model specifications to check for fakes. Pay attention to the inner wings, chassis number, boot floor, transmission tunnel, chassis rails, rear axle, dashboard and headlining.

Fakery is rife. Offside strut top shows chassis number, here (arrowed) stamped into a heavy-duty reinforcing plate (outlined). Note the washer bottle in the proper Mk2 RS position.

Interior and trim

It's not essential to the structure, but if you'd like a show car you'll need to research the original spec – returning an Escort to standard can cost thousands.

Below: Research the spec – restoring an interior to this standard is hugely expensive.

9 Serious evaluation
– 60 minutes for years of enjoyment

Score each section as follows: 4 = excellent; 3 = good; 2 = average; 1 = poor
The totting up procedure is detailed at the end of the chapter. Be realistic in your marking!

Engine

Crossflow engine

Most Mk1 and Mk2 Escorts are fitted with Ford's omnipresent Kent Crossflow engine, in 1100cc, 1300cc or 1600cc guise. All look similar, but the 1600 block is $^7/_{16}$in taller and has 711M6015BA cast onto the side rather than 711M6015AA.

Although Kent engines wear out, they're cheap, simple to fix and easy to replace. That said, with regular oil changes and an eye on maintenance, they go on forever.

Tired engines tend to be overly noisy. All are a bit harsh, but listen for excessive metallic rattling, which could point to a slack timing chain or badly-adjusted tappets. Frequent clacking suggests the tappets are broken up (possibly with matching camshaft problems, which needs an engine-out repair), but a constant typewriter-like tapping is more likely to require minor adjustments.

A high-mileage, abused or worn-out Kent will invariably show symptoms of heavy oil consumption, resulting in 'breathing' when warm – remove the oil filler cap, rev the engine and check for fumes emanating from the spout. Tired pistons, rings or cylinder bores are the most likely culprits, and will also produce blue smoke from the exhaust under load; 1100cc and 1300cc engines can suffer with piston ring problems as early as 60,000 miles. Similar smoke could also point to a dirty breather system, or fatigued valve stem seals if evident at start-up.

If a 1600cc unit has a faint knocking from cold that lessens as the engine warms, it's probably piston slap. Again, this will require a rebuild.

Crossflows are prone to oil leaks (especially from the rocker cover and sump), resulting in a grimy engine bay. Front crankshaft seals are a particular problem, although cheap and easy to replace.

Leaks cause serious problems if the oil level runs low, potentially overheating the piston skirts, crankshaft and bearings. If the car has an oil pressure gauge, make sure it doesn't drop off the scale at idle.

A tired, smoky Kent will lack power but exhibit no immediate danger of breaking down. Poor running is more likely due to a worn distributor or fuelling fault. Single-choke Motorcraft carburettors (found on most models) are particularly poor, suffering split diaphragms and worn spindles. Sporting Escorts generally have Weber twin-choke carbs instead, which also get tired; automatic choke mechanisms are notoriously prone to failure.

Finally, if you're buying a Mk1 Mexico, make sure the engine has a big-wing sump, featuring hand-welded protrusions at the back.

Breathing oil fumes from the rocker cover suggests a piston problem.

Pinto engine

RS2000s, RS Mexicos and hundreds of replicas have Pinto powerplants – identical to Cortina and Capri engines.

The Pinto is cheap, simple and relatively strong. It's also easily tuneable (many have been upgraded with bigger carburettors, Sierra cylinder blocks and so on), but there's little to worry about other than general wear.

Any Pinto needs normal used-car-buying checks for signs of head gasket failure (water in the oil, oil in the water, a heavy misfire, or white clouds from the exhaust), or symptoms of oil burning. If there's blue smoke from the exhaust, chances are it's the valve seals or a piston ring problem (eventually leading to

Twin-choke Weber carbs do the job, but auto choke mechanisms can be problematic.

cylinder bore wear), especially in a high-mileage car. Check for breathing from the oil filler cap. All these signs can mean a full rebuild is on the cards.

With the engine running, listen for tapping (or loud rattling if it's worse) from the top end. Pinto camshafts are prone to wear, particularly when oil changes have been neglected (the cam is lubricated by an oil spray bar that's easily blocked: a revised part with bigger holes is available). At best, a rattly engine may need adjustment of the valve clearances, but could mean a new cam and followers, requiring removal of the cylinder head.

At worst, knocking noises can be from an oil-starved or tired-out bottom end – again, necessitating a complete rebuild.

Check for leaks from the water pump, although it's inexpensive to replace. Make sure the timing belt has been changed recently (every two years or 25,000 miles is good advice, although the belt is unlikely to cause damage if it breaks), and, for safety's sake, ensure the front cover is in place.

The most likely problem you'll experience from a Pinto will be poor running, overfuelling or erratic idling. The usual cause is a tired Weber carburettor or faulty auto choke mechanism. Repair kits are simple to source.

A genuine RS2000 or RS Mexico engine should have an alloy sump, along with alloy engine mounts, and aluminium alternator bracket on Mk2 versions.

Twin Cam engine

Escort Twin Cams are rare, pricey, and require careful inspection before purchase. The Norfolk-built Lotus Cortina-derived engines have a special cylinder block with an 'L' cast on the side – if it's not there it's not a proper Twin Cam lump.

Lotus engines are pretty strong, but rather old and likely to have seen some action. Parts can be hard to source and rebuilds are expensive.

Look for oil leaks around the engine, especially the cam cover, front cover (which could be twisted), front and rear oil seals, head gasket and fuel pump. Leaks often mean neglect or a bad rebuild.

Twin Cams also burn oil, so check for sludge from the exhaust. Blue smoke under acceleration suggests tired piston rings, or worn valve guides if under deceleration. Blown rings can also cause the engine to breathe heavily.

Start-up should be easy and quiet – harsh clattering is probably damaged starter ring gear. A clanking cold Twin Cam could have worn big end bearings or piston slap, especially if it quietens when warm. Oil pressure at speed should be around 40psi; if not, suspect the main or big end bearings, or a duff pump.

Tapping from the top end is normal, but possibly tired tappets if the noise reduces when warm. A louder rattle could be a problem tappet or cam trouble. Burnt valves make a puffing sound similar to a blown exhaust manifold. Timing chains cause trouble, rattling when loose or screeching if tight.

Listen for a noisy water pump, notably whining or rumbling at start-up. They're prone to failure when unused and allowed to go dry, meaning a big job to fix (involving head and sump removal), unless an aftermarket kit has been added. Rock the pump's hub to check for play, and ensure it's not dripping water.

Head gasket failure is cause for concern. Look for oil mixing with water or white plumes from the exhaust and a temperature gauge that fluctuates with engine revs. If possible, check the engine's compression.

Twin Cams should idle evenly and pull smoothly. Out of tune carburettors could be to blame, but they're easy enough to overhaul.

Make sure the original airbox isn't missing – they're very pricey to replace. And try to find out whether the cylinder head has been skimmed – too much renders it scrap.

BDA engine

Not for the faint-hearted! Unless you're an engine expert, seek specialist advice before viewing any BDA-powered Escort. It's not that the engines are hugely problematic – just that they cost massive amounts to repair.

Yes, virtually all the parts are available to maintain and rebuild a BDA, but because the engines are rare and still used in motorsport, nothing is cheap. BDAs need careful servicing to keep in good shape, and were never intended for everyday motoring.

What's more, because BDAs were fitted only to RS1600s and RS1800s – the most valuable of all Escorts – it's essential that you undertake the most thorough inspection before parting with your cash.

Crucially, you need to ensure it's the real deal. Early RS1600s had 711M Crossflow cylinder blocks with the Cosworth 16-valve head, but from 1972 there was an alloy block with H721F casting number. All RS1800s contained the alloy block, but the final 50 also boasted a steel crank; these engines were numbered HRE7701 to HRE7750.

Beware any BDA that's clattery, burning oil, misfiring or showing symptoms of head gasket failure. Broken valve gear and oil leaks are relatively common, with associated pricey pitfalls.

Having said all that, no finer engine was ever fitted to an Escort, and if you can afford a BDA you'll not regret it.

Cooling system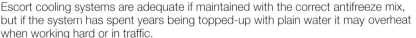

Escort cooling systems are adequate if maintained with the correct antifreeze mix, but if the system has spent years being topped-up with plain water it may overheat when working hard or in traffic.

Remove the radiator cap, checking the coolant is clean rather than a reddish-brown, rusty colour. Poor maintenance will lead to the cylinder block's water galleries getting clogged; eventually the radiator and heater matrix become blocked with flakes of rust.

Water pump impellers also suffer from corrosion, preventing the pump from circulating the coolant efficiently. Alloy thermostat housings, and the alloy unions on water pumps and inlet manifolds can also suffer corrosion.

Exhaust system 4 3 2 1

Standard systems were supplied in two different qualities, neither of which lasted very long. Genuine Ford replacements are expensive, but pattern parts are readily available – often in durable stainless steel, which is a bonus if already fitted.

Remove the radiator cap when cold to check the colour of the coolant.

Genuine RS exhaust manifold, found on Mk2 RS2000s and RS Mexicos.

GT-spec Crossflow engines had a tubular exhaust manifold, prone to cracking on the welds.

Cracked exhaust manifolds are common on sporting Kent-engined Escorts, producing a chuffing noise that increases with engine speed. Repairs are rarely successful, so a new manifold will be needed.

Mk2 RS2000s and RS Mexicos have a special cast iron exhaust manifold, complete with RS logo. If it's not there, start asking questions.

Gearbox 4 3 2 1
Manual gearbox

Most Escorts are equipped with a four-speed manual gearbox in one of three types.

The vast majority (all Kent-engined

Exhaust hanger positions reveal an Escort's identity, this being a stock non-RS Mk2 setup.

manual cars except the Mexico) use a Type 2, which is fine in 1100cc or 1300cc machines. Higher-powered models have a close-ratio version, which in the Mk2 Sport and Ghia is upgraded with stronger internals – essential if the car you're buying is tuned or fitted with a 1600cc engine.

The Mk1 Mexico, Twin Cam and RS1600 feature a 2000E gearbox, while the RS2000, RS1800 and RS Mexico use a Cortina-sourced Type E transmission.

It's wise to make sure a 2000E is the genuine item – a big, black lump of cast iron, with three-rail shift mechanism, bolt-on bellhousing, cast alloy top cover and iron tail, chrome stick and reversing light switch in a tapped hole. It's a close-ratio unit, which should be obvious on your test drive.

Similarly, an Escort RS's Type E should have an alloy bellhousing, quickshift lever, and alloy spacer blocks between the mountings and tunnel to lower the tail end. Its black, cast iron casing, alloy tail housing and pressed alloy top cover are the same on Cortinas, Capris and such like.

Manual 'boxes were quiet when new, but can be noisy now, especially if they've covered many miles. Listen for rumbling or whining, which can point to worn bearings, especially in the first three gears. They're not costly to refurbish (and they'll keep going for years) but a secondhand gearbox is generally the easiest option. Excessive noise from a 2000E could also be caused by a layshaft fault.

Crunching when changing gear may be down to synchromesh failure, but on Type 2s and Type Es it could be as simple as a stretched clutch cable.

If you can't engage a gear or there's no drive when it's selected, assume there's a bigger problem – especially if the Escort's engine has been modified. It's not unusual for excessive torque to strip gears completely.

Make sure a Type E gearbox has a firm change and doesn't jump out of gear when off-throttle – another sign of an impending rebuild.

Oh, and unless you're hot on originality, don't be too put off by a five-speed gearbox conversion – done properly, it can make an Escort a more pleasant prospect for long journeys.

Automatic gearbox

Rare but still found in several luxury-level Escorts is a three-speed automatic gearbox. Mk1s have a cable-operated Borg Warner 35, while an oil-cooled, rod-linkage Ford C3 'box is fitted to Mk2s.

Both are reliable, and the C3 does an adequate job when working properly, especially if its fluid is changed frequently. But be prepared for problems finding replacements if either gearbox causes trouble.

On the test drive, ensure gear changes are smooth and well matched to engine revs. Hesitation to change or engage drive/reverse, or clonks when downshifting, could point to problems with brake band servos or clutch pack pistons. Excessive slip under acceleration could be down to worn clutches.

But it could also signify a serious internal problem, requiring a full rebuild by a specialist. Poor acceleration from cold may be torque convertor trouble, through silt build-up or excessive wear.

Mk1 autos rely on a kick-down cable to alter shift speeds – if it's sticking, the change quality will be poor; adjustment is a specialist-only procedure.

C3 'box shift speeds are controlled by a vacuum pipe from the inlet manifold. Late changes, with excessive engine revs, suggest a split vacuum pipe, which is an easy fix.

Check an autobox for oil cleanliness – it should be red, but a brown colour or offensive smell indicates the clutch packs are failing within the 'box, requiring a costly rebuild.

Use of the correct automatic transmission fluid is critical. The wrong type or later specification fluid will cause premature gearbox failure.

Clutch ④ ③ ② ①

Most models have a cable-operated clutch, but 2000E gearboxes use an hydraulic setup with bulkhead-mounted fluid reservoir.

Clutch cables can stretch, making it difficult to select gears (especially first and reverse) but they're easy to adjust. Similar symptoms can be attributed to air in a hydraulic system – probably due to tired cylinder seals.

Clutch slip while driving (when the engine revs rise under acceleration but the car doesn't increase speed) is common, meaning a new clutch is required. Replacement means gearbox removal, but it's an easy enough job for DIY mechanics.

Difficulty engaging first and reverse may also point to a faulty clutch pressure plate, or worn-out spigot bearing in the back of the crankshaft. Clutch judder may be caused by soggy or broken engine mounts or gearbox mount, a faulty clutch or a warped flywheel.

Propshaft ④ ③ ② ①

Propshafts come in three flavours, depending on model – single-piece, two-piece with centre universal joint (UJ) and mounting, or two-piece with a centre CV joint and mounting.

Vibration or knocking from the transmission or floorpan could point to a worn-out UJ. Some early props have UJs held in with circlips (a DIY fix), but later cars need specialist attention.

The centre bearing is encased within its mounting, inside a circular rubber bushing. If the bushing fails it causes excessive movement.

Tired two-piece propshafts can cause knocking and vibration through the floorpan.

Any propshaft with too much play is cause for concern (vibration may damage the differential pinion bearings and gearbox bearings), so check around the UJs or centre mount.

Don't be tempted to drive an Escort with a worn-out propshaft – breakage can cause extreme damage.

Rear axle

4 3 2 1

The vast majority of Escorts have what's known as an English rear axle, which has a differential unit attached to the front of the casing with self-locking nuts. Less common is the Kolne axle, with a steel cover bolted to the rear of the casing (not to be confused with the heavy-duty Atlas axle found on some modified Escorts).

Rear axle whine is common; usually a result of high mileage. It's generally caused by wear in the crownwheel and pinion. Excessive backlash may be due to wear in the sun and planetary gears within the differential. The easiest/cheapest fix is to replace the entire diff, which, on an English axle, is a relatively straightforward job.

A typical non-RS Mk2 (or late-model Mk1) rear end, with English rear axle and upright telescopic dampers.

Rumbling or ticking from the axle may be due to its main diff bearings or half-shaft bearings. The latter can be replaced by a DIYer, but the former is a professional job, which, in reality, means a replacement axle is cheaper.

Make sure the differential isn't dripping with oil from its pinion seal, which can eventually lead to bearing failure if allowed to run dry: replacing the seal requires care.

Excessive torque and/or abuse can also take its toll on Escort axles, but big breakages are rare.

All AVO and RS models have a pair of radius arms on welded brackets, linking the back axle to the underbody alongside the chassis rails. None have anti-roll bar mounts on the axle casing.

Radius rods link the back axle of every Escort RS to underbody brackets.

Front suspension

4 3 2 1

MacPherson struts are fitted to the front of all Escorts, complete with coil springs and – on all but the very earliest Mk1s – an anti-roll bar. It's very straightforward to inspect.

Check the coil springs aren't broken, and make sure their cups on the struts aren't rusted through – new springs are readily available, but replacement casings are only available secondhand.

An underside inspection lets you look for play in the track control arm bushes.

Suspension towers under the front wings get flaky and rust away. Seen here is an intact non-RS model without the RS's strengthening fillets.

Rot can be rife inside the front wheelarches and around the anti-roll bar mounts.

Examine the damper inserts for leaks by looking for oil traces around the pistons. Test the shock absorbers for wear by pushing down on each front wing and seeing how soon the car settles. It it's too soft or bounces around, the dampers are tired. If it barely moves, the Escort probably has motorsport-spec suspension ...

On the test drive, a whining or rumbling noise will probably be caused by worn wheel bearings. If there are squeaking sounds and juddering over bumps, the inner track control arm bushes are probably shot; the simple resolution is to replace the whole arm, complete with standard or uprated polyurethane bushes. Knocking from the front could be due to loose or broken top mounts, or failed anti-roll bar bushes, which are cheap enough to replace.

Bear in mind RS models have an uprated anti-roll bar, strengthened front crossmember (Mk1 RS2000-onwards) and different mounts, giving obvious negative camber and front wheels that sit further back in the arches; if it looks wrong, it should ring alarm bells.

All RSs feature beefier Capri-type front struts and springs (noticeably larger than standard Escort parts), along with bolted-on steering arms, which were integral to the struts on standard cars.

Steering

Escort steering is by rack and pinion, which is simple and reliable, without power assistance. On the test drive it should feel direct and positive, with very little play –

the front road wheels should turn with minimal movement from the steering wheel, so any slack or wandering is cause for concern. A tired steering rack is the likely culprit, requiring refurbishment or replacement – not too pricey.

Steering rack gaiters sometime split and leak; worn bushes can cause play.

Play could also be due to perished mounting bushes or a split in the steering coupling's flexible rubber joint.

While you're inspecting the rack, look at the gaiters, which are prone to splitting. It's not a serious fault, but can let in dirt that will lead to deterioration of the rack.

Oh, and bear in mind that if the steering feels exceptionally heavy, the Escort may have a quick rack, needing fewer turns from lock to lock. Good for rallying, but not too friendly when parallel parking.

Rear suspension

Escort rear suspension is even simpler than the front, with a live axle, leaf springs and telescopic shock absorbers. Post-November 1973 mainstream models also feature an anti-roll bar; RS Escorts have radius rods instead, which link the axle to special brackets welded to the chassis rails – if they're not there (or there's a rear anti-roll bar in place), it's not an RS.

Rear springs are prone to sagging with age (look for the car sitting lower than standard or leaning on one side) and snapping across individual leaves. Their bushes can also become tired, so feel for soggy handling. Tired dampers may also be the cause, so inspect them externally for oil leaks. Replacements are readily available and straightforward to swap.

Inclined rear shock absorbers were fitted until November 1973.

Rear leaf springs can sag or split through entire leaves. Check the brake pipes, too.

While you're there, check for corrosion around the upper mountings, especially on post-November 1973 cars, which have upright shock absorbers poking through a crossmember in the boot floor.

Rear spring hangers

Escort rear leaf springs are fastened to a bracket at each end; all four make great muck collectors, which means they rust away with apparent delight.

If you're buying an AVO or RS model, ensure there are skidded (boxed-in) sections just in front of the forward-most rear spring hangers. Alongside them, there should also be welded brackets for radius rods, linked to the rear axle.

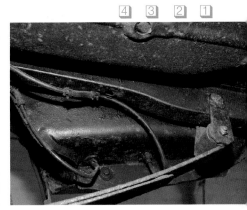

Look for corrosion all around the rear spring hangers, chassis rails and fuel tank well.

Brakes

Most surviving Escorts have a conventional setup with front discs and rear drums, but many non-sporting models wore unassisted stoppers, often with drums all round. In good order they're okay, but rarely up to the job of modern motoring. An upgrade is preferable, with front discs and servo assistance at least.

Escort braking systems have few faults, although some parts can be difficult to find. In particular, Girling servos and master cylinders from early RS models are awkward to source, and just as tricky to obtain parts for repairs.

Everything else is quite commonplace, though, including the problems you might find.

Start by casting an eye over the brake lines – metal pipes corrode, while rubber hoses perish and split. Look for fluid seeping out around the drums or callipers – wheel cylinders are particularly prone to leaking.

Brake master cylinders and servos vary between models, with some types almost impossible to find new.

Braking systems are pretty straightforward. Front discs and callipers are cheap to replace if seized or worn.

Don't be surprised to see rusty discs or feel the effect vibrating through the pedal. They're cheap to replace, but juddering can also be due to a seized calliper piston (which tends to make the car pull to one side under braking), or worn wheel bearings (which rumble when the wheels turn).

An Escort's brake pedal should feel firm but easily depressed. Too soft, and there's likely to be air in the system; too hard, and there's probably a seized cylinder.

Wheels

It sounds obvious, but if you're buying a standard car, make sure it's wearing the right wheels (without corrosion). Ford produced dozens of different wheels with similar designs, and an incorrect rim can make a big difference to the car's value.

Twin Cams and early AVO Escorts wore Lotus Cortina wheels until 1971, when slotted versions took over. In 1972 they were swapped for sports steels with a pressed spoke effect – always 5.5x13in with wide, dished rims. RS Mk2s wore this style, too.

RS four-spoke alloys are popular, but easily mistaken for cheap Capri versions. Mk1 RS alloys were 5.5x13in with a 70mm centre hole; Mk2 RS alloys were 6x13in with flat (rather than tapered) nut seats, along with an appropriate date code cast onto a spoke.

RS four-spokes are easily mistaken for cheaper Capri alloys.

Fuse box

Fuse boxes are easy to access on the passenger-side bulkhead, and also exposed to moisture. It's common to find corroded electrical contacts, bad earths and poor connections on the multi-plug that joins the car's wiring loom. The fuse box area is also a prime spot for rot.

Mk1 fuse box found on the passenger-side bulkhead. Poor connections are a common occurrence.

Wiring loom

Thanks to age and alterations, many Escorts have wiring with dodgy connections, corroded contacts and bad earths, causing issues that include failed switches and slow starting. Check the wiring loom for breaks and home-made modifications, which can make problems a nightmare to trace.

Bulkhead

A tricky place to repair but also a common spot for rot, the engine bulkhead needs careful attention.

Look for rust around the bulkhead heater dome, which gets clogged with dirt and corrodes from the inside out. Alongside and beneath the dome, the seam between the bulkhead's horizontal and vertical panels can split or rot severely.

On the upper bulkhead, check around the fuse box and bonnet hinge plates for rust holes or stress-cracks; rectification is tricky. Mk2 Ghia/RS2000 insulation pads make great water traps, so lift it to check underneath. Make sure it's not damaged either – good replacements are rare.

Lower down, keep looking for rust – especially alongside the chassis legs and floorpan uprights, which can rot through to the cabin – and use this area to ensure you're buying a genuine model. Sporty Mk1s and RS Mk2s have a factory-drilled hole for an oil pressure pipe, while MK1s with hydraulic clutches have no clutch cable tube on the pedal box reinforcing plate, or a blanked-off section over the tube end instead.

Note that early Mk1s have smaller bonnet hinge supports, and lack the later Escorts' heater dome end cutouts (the dome is a complete curve) with washer nozzles running up each side (rather than poking through the bonnet). Pre-February 1977 Mk2s have five square dimples where the bulkhead joins the scuttle panel, with seven thereafter.

Bulkheads rot badly – as shown by this Mk2's fuse box area.

Bonnet hinge supports rot away or suffer stress fractures around the welds.

Inner wings

④ ③ ② ①

Escort inner wings are a good pointer to the car's overall condition – if they're nice and solid, chances are the rest of the car will be good too.

Most obvious are the MacPherson strut upper mounting points, which seemingly began to rust as soon as cars left the factory. In severe cases, the suspension struts collapse, pushing through the inner wings and into the bonnet.

Don't be put off by an Escort that's been welded in this area (the vast majority have) but be cautious of careless welding (which could distort the suspension geometry), signs of bubbling or repair plates applied over grot.

Don't, of course, mistake repairs for AVO/RS suspension top reinforcing plates, which were neatly spot-welded to all such sporty models (plus all heavy-duty bodyshells). If you're inspecting such a heavy-duty shell (including AVO and RS models), look underneath the wheelarch, which should have reinforcing plates in the suspension towers, along with strengthening fillets at the top, adjoining the inner wings.

All Escorts can suffer corrosion in the vertical braces of the front suspension

Typically corroded strut tops, as plated over in the 1970s. A restored car should be somewhat tidier ...

Slam panel edges are a prime spot for rot. This is an early Mk2.

towers, which can be hidden by dirt and underseal – it's best to remove both front wheels to check.

Look at the tops of the inner wings too – the drip rails rot through, spreading to nearby panels. Examine the battery tray for corrosion, likewise inspecting the bonnet slam panel, especially above the headlamps.

Finally, double-check the vertical seams where the inner wings attach to the bulkhead – terminal rot in this area can result in the car literally folding up.

Chassis

Severe chassis rot used to be terminal for Escorts, and it's still a serious concern – so support the car and check underneath very carefully.

A pair of chassis rails run the entire length of an Escort, and every inch can dissolve – so you'll need to inspect the rails from front to back, on all three visible faces of the box sections, plus above if possible (by lifting the carpets inside).

Ensure none of the drain holes have become enlarged, and beware of any suspicious-looking underseal. Make sure, too, that the rails haven't detached from where they're welded to the floorpan.

Chassis rails require careful inspection for corrosion – here within the rear wheelarches.

Your search for corrosion should be thorough – here are the front chassis rails as viewed from underneath.

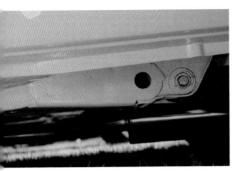

RS chassis rails have boxed-in sections just in front of the rear spring hangers.

A non-RS model's chassis rails and forward-most rear spring hangers – an ideal place to spot the rot.

There's no one area of chassis that's more prone to corrosion than the rest (it's all a potential nightmare), but pay particular attention to the front anti-roll bar mounts and chassis leg swan necks beneath the engine bay, which quickly swell with rust.

Needless to say, signs of crumpled or distorted box sections could point to accident damage.

Sills

An Escort killer since time began, rust appeared on many cars' sills when they were little more than a year old. You'll need to prod and poke the inner and outer sills everywhere – front to back, under the car and beneath the carpets. Check the outriggers at the backs of the Mk2 sills, too – it's unusual to see them intact.

Sills are structural, so holes are a no-no; beware of any bubbling and be cautious of bad welding or body filler.

Rusty sills aren't the end of the world because replacements are cheap and readily available. But if an Escort has been neglected in this area, it's a danger sign for the rest of the car's condition.

It's essential to check sills for rot, which can be trapped and hidden behind some models' decorative trims.

Some models – including the Super, GT and 1300E – have decorative trim along the outer sills. Not only does it quicken the rusting process, it makes a good job of hiding corrosion. Be sure to examine these areas extra-carefully.

Floors

It's vital to inspect as much of an Escort's floorpan as possible, from above and below.

Inside you'll need to lift the carpet, paying attention to the front footwells and kick panels beneath the dashboard at each side (which tend to rot out thanks to leaks from the windscreen) and front seat supports. Corrosion eventually spreads

to and from the inner sills, plus the rear floorpans and seat belt mounts, too. It's also wise to check the floors, transmission tunnel and rear crossmember for stress-cracks through the welds, especially on modified cars.

Ensuring it's supported securely, have a thorough poke around beneath the car. Holes will be obvious but copious underseal can disguise lots of rot. Just take your time, and press or tap anything that looks flaky.

Not pretty but strong enough – a plate has been welded to the front footwell (seen from underneath) to repair/replace a corroded section.

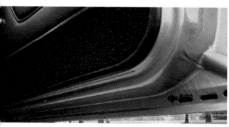

Doors

Check for rust along the door bottoms, which rot where the skin attaches, often from the inside out. Doors also corrode spectacularly around the frames, especially underneath and around the hinges. Use a magnet to search for hidden filler on the outer face, and make sure there aren't any badly-executed repairs or ill-aligned skins.

Door frames can disintegrate – it's rare to find a bottom this good ...

Doors may also drop when they're opened (especially on two-door models), so check by jiggling them from their rear edges. New hinge pins (a cheap job) will probably cure the sagging, but make sure movement isn't coming from rot in the A-pillar or flexing from the door itself.

Door A-pillars

Escorts rot badly in the A-pillars around the hinges, with rust bubbling through from the inner wheelarches. Repairs are tricky, and it's common to find filler instead of solid metal. Beware!

Rotten door pillars are bad news, requiring tricky repairs.

Front panel

Look for rust around the headlamp bowls, across the front valance (behind the spoiler, if fitted) and on the seams where the front panel joins the wings. Also peer behind

Check the front panel's seams where it attaches to the wings.

the front panel where it's welded to the radiator support crossmember – another prime place to spot rot.

Front wings ⁴ ³ ² ¹

Rust appears at each corner of the front wings – on the leading edges around and above the headlights, lower down where they attach to the front panel, in the top corners beside the windscreen scuttle, and their lower edges behind the front wheels and against the sills, gradually spreading all the way to the top. Check for rot all along their drip rails where they join the inner wings too.

Mk1 Twin Cam, Mexico, RS1600, RS2000, Sport and 1300E have flared front wheelarches and correspondingly high-priced replacement wings – when you can find them.

Good reproduction Mk2 wings are available, and identical throughout the range – except for the RS2000, which has unique front wings and associated replacement costs.

Bonnet ⁴ ³ ² ¹

Escort bonnets rust across the front – especially at each corner – and the skin underneath, where the latch attaches. The entire underside is also prone to corrosion, eventually necessitating a complete replacement. Good Mk1 bonnets are rare, but repro Mk2 parts are reasonably priced. That's except for Mk2 RS2000 bonnets, which are unique and unavailable new – although fibreglass replicas can be fitted (but beware, because they're also found on some RS replicas).

Scuttle panel ⁴ ³ ² ¹

A top spot for rot or filler, and a bad sign if it's present. Check carefully across the scuttle panel beneath the windscreen, especially where it meets the front wings and windscreen pillars.

The scuttle panel rots beneath the windscreen. Rust works its way up the roof pillars.

B-pillars and C-pillars ⁴ ³ ² ¹

Rot can appear where the pillars attach to the back wings, and Mk2 C-pillars in particular can be a real nightmare. Two-door Mk2s are especially prone to corrosion beneath the rear side windows, thanks to blocked drain channels.

Rot here can be very tricky to repair, and often points to a bodyshell that's poor in plenty of other places.

Two-door Mk2s are prone to rotting at the base of the C-pillars.

Boot lid [4] [3] [2] [1]

Check the underside of the boot lid, which rusts around the double-skinned section. Also look at the rear wings around the boot aperture, checking there's no corrosion or filler, especially in the panel beneath the rear windscreen.

Boot lid and rear wings showing terminal corrosion.

Rear wheelarches [4] [3] [2] [1]

Rear wheelarches rot out, spreading upwards from the arch lips, eating the rear wings. Rust also attacks the inner arches – on two-door cars they're hard to inspect without the rear wheel removed, but on four-door models you'll see corrosion when you open the rear doors.

Rot continues along the bottoms of the rear wings, and it's common to find filler on the lower corners where they meet the spare wheel/fuel tank well.

Pay particular attention to the wheelarches on early Supers and GTs, which have chrome beading around the edges, trapping muck and leading to more rust.

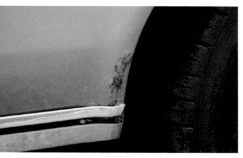 

Rear wheelarches bubble up before rusting all the way around their lips and spreading to the sills (shown here).

Inner wheelarches can completely rot away, but four-door rears are easy to inspect.

Rear panel [4] [3] [2] [1]

Serious rot can occur around the back lights (especially on Mk1s with chrome 'hockey sticks'), near the bumper irons and chassis rail end sections, in the seam adjoining the boot, all across the rear valance, and the seam where the panel meets the back wings.

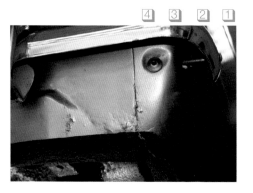

The rear valance rusts and splits beneath the back bumper irons.

Roof

Windscreen pillars can rust from the bottom upwards, as can the drip rails, which rot away beneath their chrome (or plastic-chrome on later cars) trims. Any corrosion should be evident along the gutters themselves.

Escort roofs are generally good unless a vinyl covering has been fitted. Aftermarket versions retain moisture, while factory-fitted Mk2 vinyls can be worse because they were applied to primer rather than topcoat. Splits or lifting of the vinyl should be inspected carefully – it's safe to assume there will be rust underneath.

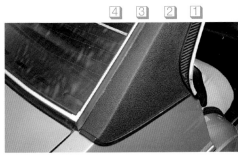

Splits in vinyl roofs allow moisture to settle on the metal, eventually leading to serious corrosion.

Oh, and if the car has a sunroof, try to decide if it's something you can live with. An authentic roll-back Webasto needn't affect an Escort's value, but many owners dislike pop-up glass sunroofs.

Brightwork

The chrome-plated components on Escorts are often pitted, but can be rechromed for a reasonable cost. Just be sure that the parts are correct for the car because some can be expensive – for example, a straight Mk1 back bumper (without central cutout) or front quarter bumpers.

Rubbing strips along Mk2 flanks and chrome beading around some Mk1 models' boot lids and window surrounds act as a perfect place for moisture to sit. The brightwork is clipped into place, so not only can it become pitted, the bodywork underneath will start to rust – in some cases quite dramatically.

Sporty Mk2s are generally equipped

Brightwork around the boot lid is a common moisture trap – leading to corrosion.

with satin black rather than chromed parts, but they're equally prone to corroding. Genuine replacements are pricey, but modern reproductions are easier on the wallet.

Badges and decals

Don't be put off by an Escort with poor-condition badges or decals – almost everything is available as a good-quality repro, but if you're determined to search for genuine Ford replacements you could be waiting a long, long time.

Spoilers

Mk2 rubber rear spoilers suffer splits and cracks, and replacements aren't available new – so expect to pay heavily for a genuine part. Proper polyurethane Mk2 front spoilers and RS2000 snouts are similarly scarce, although fibreglass repros are around. Don't be put off by early RS Mexicos and RS1800s with fibreglass front spoilers; some are genuine.

Boot spoilers sometimes split, and good replacements cost a fortune. Repro badges and stickers aren't a problem.

Windows

Several types of glass were fitted to Escorts, with varying degrees of current availability. Clear glass was found in everyday models, and can be tricky to find new. Green tints were in luxury-spec Mk2s (including some RSs) until 1978, and very tricky to source. The bronze tints of later cars are nigh on irreplaceable.

Opening front quarter lights are rare (read pricey), and Mk1 opening rear side windows tended to fall out when the adhesive failed. Consider it a bonus if they're present and fully-functioning.

Window rubbers

Check the window rubbers for perishing – a common occurrence. Reproduction replacements of most types are available off the shelf (not especially cheaply), but bear in mind what damage might have been caused by leaks, especially from around the windscreen.

Headlamps

Most everyday Escorts wore sealed-beam headlamps, which were never particularly effective even when new. Far better are the halogen lights found on higher-spec models.

Window rubbers split, but repros are available new.

All headlamps corrode, as do their metal headlamp bowls, which rot away from behind.

Authentic halogen units are rare, and headlamps for some AVO cars can be eye-wateringly expensive. Mk2 RS2000 lamps can be hit-and-miss, with genuine inners available and outer units rather rare.

Light clusters

Faulty rear lamps or front indicators are generally caused by bad connections,

Genuine headlamps can be hard to source, and Mk2 RS2000 Cibié units are no exception.

poor earths and corroded bodies. Genuine replacements are hard to find, but repro lenses and complete units are available off the shelf.

Dashboard

A common place to spot an Escort that's not quite what it's making out to be, the metal dashboard has a few differences between models. Although it's possible to cut out and weld a dashboard into a car, most fakers don't go to such an extent.

Early Mk1s (pre-1970) have larger switch holes and a chrome-finished heater control; the Twin Cam and GT's headlamp switch is on the fascia, rather than under the instruments.

What should be behind the dials of any AVO or RS Mk1 – not something hacked in with an angle grinder.

All Twin Cam and AVO Escorts have six-dial instrumentation, as do GTs, most Sports and many XLs. Behind the clocks is a collection of factory-pressed cutouts, so ask the seller if it's okay to remove the pod and take a look – if it's been hacked out with an angle grinder, the bodyshell has some explaining to do!

Similarly, pre-1978 Mk2 RS2000s, RS2000 Customs and RS1800 Customs have a glove pocket recessed into the dashboard, in front of the passenger seat – you'll need to remove the two screws and look behind the pod to ensure the dashboard cutout was properly pressed by Ford. Accept no excuses …

Instruments

Gauges are generally trouble-free, with only blown bulbs or bad connections to worry about. But they're very easy to swap, so faulty units are often replaced with lower-mileage alternatives. Plastic-chrome finish wears off Mk1 binnacles and they're not available new. Excellent-condition early AVO instruments are extremely expensive.

Heater

Check the heater/demister blower works – it's not unknown for the motor to seize, meaning a fiddly fascia-out job to replace it.

Escort instruments are usually trouble-free, but winding back the odometer is a simple task – so don't assume it's correct.

Heater motors sometimes seize, so check the blower to make sure it works.

Interior trim

It's easy to throw four-figure sums at an Escort interior, simply to retrim the seats in authentic material – so bear it in mind if you're looking for a show car.

While the vinyl of most Mk1s and basic Mk2s is available (at a price), several Mk2 fabrics are impossible to source. Black Beta cloth (found in many RS models) has been reproduced, giving an almost authentic appearance. Sadly, other colours are lagging behind.

Still, Escort interiors are relatively durable, mainly suffering from the driver's seat having tears and splits in the upholstery, and collapsed springs in the bottom cushion. Sports seats wear out on the side bolsters, rear seats deteriorate across the top of the backrest, and some fabric covers (notably Beta) looked quite saggy even when new.

Seats can, of course, be rebuilt but some types (such as genuine AVO buckets) are very expensive to replace. If originality is your thing, try to research the correct specification of the model you're buying well in advance, because swapping parts at a later date can involve huge financial outlay.

Custom and Ghia door cards were the same style, and are now rare to find in immaculate condition.

Carpets wear out, especially in the driver's footwell. Repros are available.

Check the dashboard top for cracks – good replacements are very expensive.

Seat base springs collapse or poke through the upholstery. Replacement vinyl is available, although costly.

Rocker switches in the dashboard can fall apart, but are relatively cheap and easy to swap.

The padded vinyl dashboard tops in all cars can crack; good replacements for six-dial Mk1s are rare and pricey. It's the same story with door cards – especially full-height RS2000/Custom types – so beware if there are speaker holes cut in.

Likewise, genuine RS centre consoles are easily damaged or hacked around, and costly to put right.

Check the carpets for holes (very common), and be prepared to spend money sourcing a good-quality replacement. The rubber mats of basic Mk1s are even scarcer.

Headlinings can look tatty but repros are readily available (if tricky to fit). Bear in mind genuine Mexicos, most RS1600s and RS1800s, RS Mexicos and all RS2000s until 1978 have a black headlining rather than the putty colour of regular cars.

Luggage compartment

A clean, tidy and original boot floor is often the sign of a good Escort bodyshell. Early cars tend to be better than later (post-1973) versions, but all can rot right though, thanks to leaking boot lid seals, bunged-up drain holes and corrosion spreading from underneath.

The main boot floor should match the car's exterior colour, without signs of rust. All Mk1 Twin Cams, RS1600s, Mexicos, RS2000s and early Sports have eight bolts poking through the floor for a stone guard, fitted underneath to some cars.

On Twin Cams, RS1600s and pre-1973 Mexicos, one long bolt is used to retain the spare wheel, with a special bracket spot-welded to the floor alongside. Such cars have a battery on a tray in the nearside wheel well, with no tray under the bonnet.

Similarly, the Mk2 RS and Harrier have a special spare wheel strap bracket spot-welded to the boot floor alongside the spare wheel well (standard cars have a bracket in the well).

Check the spare wheel well inside the luggage compartment – most have rotted away and been replaced by now.

Check any Escort for rot in the spare wheel well and underneath the fuel tank, which is common and relatively easy to repair.

Finally, remember that only post-October 1973 Escorts have shock absorbers poking through the boot floor on a crossmember behind the back seat.

Evaluation procedure
Add up the total points.
Score: 172 = excellent (possibly concours); 129 = good; 86 = average; 43 = poor.
Cars scoring over 120 will be completely usable and will require only maintenance and care to preserve condition. Cars scoring between 43 and 88 will require some serious work or full restoration. Cars scoring between 89 and 119 will require very careful assessment of the necessary repair/restoration costs in order to arrive at a realistic value.

10 Auctions
– sold! Another way to buy your dream

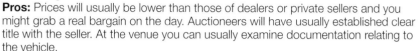

Auction pros & cons

Pros: Prices will usually be lower than those of dealers or private sellers and you might grab a real bargain on the day. Auctioneers will have usually established clear title with the seller. At the venue you can usually examine documentation relating to the vehicle.

Cons: You have to rely on a sketchy catalogue description of condition and history. The opportunity to inspect is limited and you cannot drive the car. Auction cars are often a little below par and may require some work. It's easy to overbid. There will usually be a buyer's premium to pay in addition to the auction hammer price.

Which auction?

Auctions by established auctioneers are advertised in car magazines and on the auction houses' websites. A catalogue or a simple printed list of the lots for auctions might only be available a day or two ahead, though often lots are listed and pictured on auctioneers' websites much earlier. Contact the auction company to ask if previous auction selling prices are available, as this is useful information (details of past sales are often displayed on websites).

Catalogue, entry fee and payment details

When you purchase the catalogue of the vehicles in the auction, it often acts as a ticket allowing two people to attend the viewing days and the auction. Catalogue details tend to be comparatively brief, but will include information such as 'one owner from new, low mileage, full service history,' etc. It will also usually show a guide price to give you some idea of what to expect to pay and state what is charged as a 'buyer's premium,' plus it will contain details of acceptable forms of payment. At the fall of the hammer an immediate deposit is usually required, the balance payable within 24 hours. If the plan is to pay by cash, there may be a cash limit. Some auctions will accept payment by debit card. Sometimes credit or charge cards are acceptable, but will often incur an extra charge. A bank draft or bank transfer will have to be arranged in advance with your own bank as well as with the auction house. No car will be released before all payments are cleared. If delays occur in payment transfers then storage costs can accrue.

Buyer's premium

A buyer's premium will be added to the hammer price: don't forget this in your calculations. It is not usual for there to be a further state tax or local tax on the purchase price and/or on the buyer's premium.

Viewing

In some instances it's possible to view on the day, or days before, as well as in the hours prior to, the auction. Occasionally there are auction officials available who are willing to help out by opening engine and luggage compartments and to allow you to inspect the interior. While the officials may start the engine for you, a test drive is out of the question. Crawling under and around the car as much as you want is permitted, but you can't suggest that the car you are interested in be jacked up, or attempt to do the job yourself. You can also ask to see any documentation available.

Bidding

Before you take part in the auction, decide your maximum bid – and stick to it!

It may take a while for the auctioneer to reach the lot you are interested in, so use that time to observe how other bidders behave. When it's the turn of your car, attract the auctioneer's attention and make an early bid – but not too early, or you'll risk inflating price. The auctioneer will then look to you for a reaction every time another bid is made. Usually the bids will be in fixed increments until the bidding slows, when smaller increments will often be accepted before the hammer falls. If you want to withdraw from the bidding, make sure the auctioneer understands your intentions – a vigorous shake of the head when he or she looks to you for the next bid should do the trick!

Assuming you are the successful bidder, the auctioneer will note your card or paddle number, and from that moment on you will be responsible for the vehicle.

If the car is unsold, either because it failed to reach the reserve or because there was little interest, it may be possible to negotiate with the owner, via the auctioneers, after the sale is over.

Successful bid

There are two more items to think about: how to get the car home, and insurance. If you can't drive the car, your own or a hired trailer is one way; another is to have the vehicle shipped using the facilities of a local company. The auction house will also have details of companies specialising in the transfer of cars.

Insurance for immediate cover can usually be purchased on site, but it may be more cost-effective to make arrangements with your own insurance company in advance, and then call to confirm the full details.

eBay and other online auctions

eBay and other online auctions could land you a car at a bargain price, though you'd be foolhardy to bid without examining the car first – something most vendors encourage. A useful feature of eBay is that the geographical location of the car is shown, so you can narrow your choices to those within a realistic radius of home. Be prepared to be outbid in the last few moments of the auction. Remember, your bid is binding and that it will be very, very difficult to get restitution in the case of a crooked vendor fleecing you – caveat emptor!

Be aware that some cars offered for sale in online auctions are 'ghost' cars. Don't part with any cash without being sure that the vehicle does actually exist and is as described (usually pre-bidding inspection is possible).

Auctioneers

Barrett-Jackson www.barrett-jackson.com **Barons** www.barons-auctions.com **Bonhams** www.bonhams.com **British Car Auctions (BCA)** www.bca-europe.com or www.british-car-auctions.co.uk **Cheffins** www.cheffins.co.uk **Christies** www.christies.com **Coys** www.coys.co.uk **eBay** www.ebay.com **H&H** www.classic-auctions.co.uk **RM** www.rmauctions.com **Shannons** www.shannons.com.au **Silver** www.silverauctions.com

11 Paperwork
– correct documentation is essential!

The paper trail

Classic, collector and prestige cars usually come with a large portfolio of paperwork accumulated and passed on by a succession of proud owners. This documentation represents the real history of the car and from it can be deduced the level of care the car has received, how much it's been used, which specialists have worked on it and the dates of major repairs

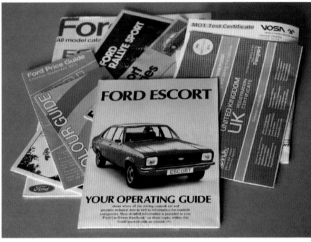

A history file and a pile of paperwork can give peace of mind.

and restorations. All of this information will be priceless to you as the new owner, so be very wary of cars with little paperwork to support their claimed history.

Registration documents

All countries/states have some form of registration for private vehicles, whether it's like the American 'pink slip' system or the British 'log book' system.

It's essential to check that the registration document is genuine, that it relates to the car in question, and that all the vehicle's details are correctly recorded, including chassis/VIN and engine numbers (if these are shown). If you are buying from the previous owner, his or her name and address will be recorded in the document; this will not be the case if you are buying from a dealer.

In the UK the current (Euro-aligned) registration document is named V5C, and is printed in coloured sections of blue, green and pink. The blue section relates to the car specification, the green section has details of the new owner and the pink section is sent to the DVLA in the UK when the car is sold. A small section in yellow deals with selling the car within the motor trade.

In the UK the DVLA will provide details of earlier keepers of the vehicle upon payment of a small fee, and much can be learned in this way.

If the car has a foreign registration, there may be expensive and time-consuming formalities to complete. Do you really want the hassle?

Roadworthiness certificate

Most country/state administrations require that vehicles are regularly tested to prove that they are safe to use on the public highway and do not produce excessive emissions. In the UK that test (the 'MoT') is carried out at approved testing stations, for a fee. In the USA the requirement varies, but most states insist on an emissions test every two years as a minimum, while the police are charged with pulling over unsafe-looking vehicles.

In the UK the test is required on an annual basis once a vehicle becomes three years old. Of particular relevance for older cars is that the certificate issued includes the mileage reading recorded at the test date and, therefore, becomes an independent record of that car's history. Ask the seller if previous certificates are available. Without an MoT the vehicle should be trailered to its new home, unless you insist that a valid MoT is part of the deal (not such a bad idea this, as at least you will know the car was roadworthy on the day it was tested, and you don't need to wait for the old certificate to expire before having the test done).

Road licence

The administration of every country/state charges some kind of tax for the use of its road system, the actual form of the 'road licence' and how it is displayed varying enormously country to country and state to state.

Whatever the form of the 'road licence,' it must relate to the vehicle carrying it and must be present and valid if the car is to be driven on the public highway legally. The value of the licence will depend on the length of time it will continue to be valid.

In the UK if a car is untaxed because it has not been used for a period of time, the owner has to inform the licensing authorities, otherwise the vehicle's date-related registration number will be lost and there will be a painful amount of paperwork to get it re-registered. Also in the UK, vehicles built before the end of 1972 (1973 from April 2014) are provided with 'tax discs' free of charge, but they must still display a valid disc. Using your chassis number, car clubs can often provide formal proof that a particular Mk1 Escort qualifies for this valuable concession, even if it was registered in 1973.

Certificates of authenticity

For many makes of collectible car it is possible to get a certificate proving the age and authenticity, but it's unlikely you'll find anything of the kind to accompany a humble Ford Escort. If you want to obtain more details of a car's history, the relevant owners' club is the best starting point – some models of Escort (mainly AVO cars and RSs) have a relevant club registrar, who may already have details of your potential purchase on file.

If the car has been used in European classic car rallies it may have a FIVA (Federation Internationale des Vehicules Anciens) certificate. The so-called FIVA Passport or FIVA Vehicle Identity Card enables organisers and participants to recognise whether or not a particular vehicle is suitable for individual events. If you want to obtain such a certificate go to www.fbhvc.co.uk or www.fiva.org. There will be similar organisations in other countries too.

Valuation certificate

Hopefully, the vendor will have a recent valuation certificate, or letter signed by a recognised expert stating how much he, or she, believes the particular car to be worth (such documents, together with photos, are usually needed to get 'agreed value' insurance). Generally, such documents should act only as confirmation of your own assessment of the car rather than a guarantee of value. The easiest way to find out how to obtain a formal valuation is to contact the relevant owners' club, which will usually need to see an Escort in the metal before issuing a valuation.

Service history

Old Escorts have often been serviced at home by enthusiastic (and hopefully capable) owners for a good number of years. Nevertheless, try to obtain as much service history and other paperwork pertaining to the car as you can. Naturally, dealer stamps or specialist garage receipts score most points in the value stakes. However, anything helps in the great authenticity game – items like the original bill of sale, handbook, parts invoices and repair bills add to the story and the character of the car. Even a brochure correct to the year of the car's manufacture is a useful document and something that you could well have to search hard to locate in future years. If the seller claims that the car has been restored, then expect receipts and other evidence from a specialist restorer.

If the seller claims to have carried out regular servicing, ask what work was completed, when, and seek some evidence of it being carried out. Your assessment of the car's overall condition should tell you whether the seller's claims are genuine.

Restoration photographs

If the seller tells you that the Escort has been restored, expect to be shown a series of photographs taken while the restoration was under way. Pictures at various stages, and from various angles, should help you gauge the thoroughness of the work. If you buy the car, ask if you can have all the photographs, as they form an important part of the vehicle's history. It's surprising how many sellers are happy to part with their car and accept your cash, but want to hang on to their photographs. If that's the case, you may be able to persuade the vendor to get a set of copies made.

12 What's it worth?
– let your head rule your heart

Condition

If the car you've been looking at is in really bad shape, you've probably not bothered to use the marking system in chapter 9 – 60 minute evaluation. You may not have even got as far as using that chapter at all!

If you did use the marking system in chapter 9, you'll know whether the car is in Excellent (maybe Concours), Good, Average or Poor condition or, perhaps, somewhere in-between these categories.

Many classic car magazines run a regular price guide. If you haven't bought the latest editions, do so now and compare their suggested values for the model you are thinking of buying; also look at the auction prices they're reporting.

Values have been fairly stable for some time, but some models will always be more sought-after than others. Trends can change too. The values published in the magazines tend to vary from one magazine to another, as do their scales of condition, so read carefully the guidance notes they provide. Of course, a truly outstanding example or a recent show winner could be worth more than the highest scale published. Bear in mind, too, that magazine estimates for Escorts are often notoriously low.

Assuming that the car you have in mind is not in Concours condition, then relate the level of condition that you judge the car to be in with the appropriate guide price. How does the figure compare with the asking price? Before you start haggling with the seller, consider what effect any variation from standard specification might have on the car's value.

If you are buying from a dealer, remember there will be a dealer's premium on the price.

Desirable options/extras

There's something for everyone in the Escort world, so buyers tend to choose their car based on model, colour, condition and extent of modifications (if any), rather than exact specification. As such, we enter the purchasing process with a preconceived plan of what the car should be like, and any extras are a bonus (or not, as the case may be …).

For example, when picking a Mk2 Ghia, we expect luxury trim and subtle paintwork; if we wanted a full-blown rally monster we'd look elsewhere. Similarly, the buyer of a sedate 1100L in dark blue won't be in the market for bright yellow RS2000 with wide wheelarches and Cosworth engine conversion. Yet that doesn't necessarily make either car more desirable than the other. Think of it like this: would you prefer a plush Mk1 Mexico with Custom Pack and optional RS alloys, or an early Mex with rubber mats and hubcaps? Each car has its well-deserved following, so you must study the different variants before starting your search.

That said, certain specifications and levels of originality always attract a strong audience – and accordingly higher prices …

• Factory specification – correct parts for the model and year.
• Matching numbers – not just the chassis plates, strut top stamping and engine numbers, but it's also desirable if markings on components (eg wheels and windows) are the right age for the car.

• Period modifications – especially official Ford Rallye Sport parts, eg an RS2000 with Group One airbox or Mexico with map reading lamp.
• Road tax exemption – Escorts manufactured before 31 December 1972 (1973 from April 2014) are entitled to free UK road fund licence.
• Colour – you can't argue against well-loved themes like a Sunset Red Mexico with white stripes, a Purple Velvet 1300E, and so on.
• Properly engineered, modern modifications – particularly for high performance or historic motorsport use.

Undesirable features
While most changes to an Escort are matters of taste, some specifications or alterations detract from a car's appeal ...
• Sunroof – a no-no for motorsport, and usually undesirable for a road car. Although an authentic dealer-fitted Webasto can add to a Mk1's value, an aftermarket glass pop-up sunroof is a negative in any Escort.
• Poorly-executed modifications – hacked-about engine swaps, customised interiors and such like.

Monster modifications – like this Cosworth YB engine conversion – are very desirable when well executed.

• Suspicious identity – mismatched history (especially hints of a fake or ringer) has a seriously detrimental effect on value.
• Incorrect specification – when a relatively standard Escort doesn't retain its factory specification (eg the wrong seats for the model year or late badges on an early car).
• Cosmetic modifications – almost anything except RS spoilers, Series X kit or rally arches on the right car.

Sunroofs can decrease an Escort's value, but an authentic Webasto shouldn't have too much affect.

• Unusual paint schemes – some colours are rare for a reason! That said, previously undesirable shades (eg browns and beiges) have seen a recent upsurge in popularity.

Striking a deal
Negotiate on the basis of your condition assessment, mileage, and fault rectification cost. Also take into account the car's specification. Be realistic about the value, but don't be completely intractable: a small compromise on the part of the vendor or buyer will often facilitate a deal at little real cost.

Taking on someone else's half-started project can mean a world of troubles ...

Make no mistake, Ford Escorts were built as basic run-of-the-mill machines by a company renowned for its cost-cutting skills, through times of deep turmoil in the manufacturing industry. Regardless of L badges or RS stripes, they were little more than disposable objects, and many began rusting almost as soon as they left the production line.

Now, several decades later, it's amazing any Escorts have survived. So unless you buy a concours car from the top of the market, chances are an Escort will require some improvement. The question is, how much?

A basket-case Escort in need of complete restoration is pretty easy to appraise. It will probably call for huge amounts of welding, new panels, paintwork, engine, transmission and running gear repairs. Not to mention countless pieces of hard-to-find trim and expensive interior reupholstering.

Are you capable of tackling it all? Most of an Escort's mechanicals are very basic and easy to work on, but bodywork can be tricky to get right. You should also be prepared to spend far longer than anticipated to perfect your project, meanwhile scouring the country for exactly the right components.

If you're instead considering a professional restoration, expect to spend more than the car's eventual value to achieve the best results. Rebuilding a desirable model may just about yield a profit, but bear in mind many pricey components (such as body panels) are shared across the Escort range – so a pro rebuild of a four-door Popular could almost equal that of an RS1800 ...

On the positive side, restoring (and even reshelling) an Escort from scratch means you get to choose the exact specification, colour scheme, and quality of the finished item. If you've got the budget and intend to keep the car indefinitely, it's probably the most satisfying prospect.

In almost all cases, a project with tired mechanicals (unless you've got a broken BDA engine) will be cheaper to repair than, say, a bodily rotten Escort.

A half-restored or average-condition Escort is harder to pigeonhole; an apparently nicely-painted car could be full of filler, and those just-need-finishing details could be impossible to source. In the worst-case scenario, you may even decide to redo the previous owner's work or some items you previously thought were acceptable – in which case, you're simply buying a major renovation project but paying more for it from the outset.

One good point, though, is that a roadworthy Escort can be enjoyed as a rolling restoration, and it's viable to rebuild many parts at your leisure while keeping the car usable. That said, it's not generally the best way to get great results.

All things considered, there's a lot to be said for choosing an excellent or concours condition Escort, if you can afford the initial outlay. All the better if you're already familiar with the car, it's an original example, or comes with good-quality restoration photos.

Worth restoring? When an Escort's this far gone, rebuild costs will most likely outweigh its eventual value.

14 Paint problems
– bad complexion, including dimples, pimples and bubbles

Paint faults generally occur due to lack of protection/maintenance, or to poor preparation prior to a respray or touch-up. All Escort paints can be easily matched, but modern finishes may look out of place on a Mk1 or Mk2. Some of the following conditions may be present in the car you're looking at.

Orange peel
This appears as an uneven paint surface, similar to the appearance of the skin of an orange. The fault is caused by the failure of atomized paint droplets to flow into each other when they hit the surface. It's sometimes possible to rub out the effect with proprietary paint cutting/rubbing compound or very fine grades of abrasive paper. A respray may be necessary in severe cases. Remember, though, that Ford's factory finish had more than its fair share of orange peel, and on a concours car this appearance is considered desirable.

Cracking
Severe cases are likely to have been caused by too heavy an application of paint (or filler beneath the paint). Also, insufficient stirring of the paint before application can lead to the components being improperly mixed, and cracking can result. Incompatibility with the paint already on the panel can have a similar effect. To rectify the problem it is necessary to rub down to a smooth, sound finish before respraying the affected area.

Crazing
Sometimes the paint takes on a crazed rather than a cracked appearance when the problems mentioned under 'Cracking' are present. This problem can also be caused by a reaction between the underlying surface and the paint. Paint removal and respraying the problem area is usually the only solution.

Rust bubbles – about to burst.

Blistering
Almost always caused by corrosion of the metal beneath the paint. Usually perforation will be found in the metal and the damage will often be worse than that suggested by the area of blistering. The metal will have to be repaired before repainting.

Micro blistering
Usually the result of an economy respray, where

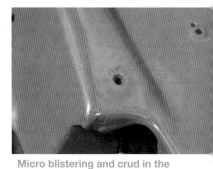

Micro blistering and crud in the top coat.

inadequate heating has allowed moisture to settle on the car before spraying.

Consult a paint specialist, but usually damaged paint will have to be removed before partial or full respraying. Can also be caused by car covers that don't 'breathe.'

Fading
Some colours, especially reds, are prone to fading if subjected to strong sunlight for long periods without the benefit of polish protection. Sometimes proprietary paint restorers and/or paint cutting/rubbing compounds will retrieve the situation. Often a respray is the only real solution.

Peeling
A common problem with early Ford metallic paintwork, when single-layer paints had adhesion problems. Modern sealing lacquers also become damaged and peel off, while poorly-applied paint can peel too. The remedy is to strip and start again.

Dimples
Dimples in the paintwork are caused by the residue of polish (particularly silicone types) not being removed properly before respraying. Paint removal and repainting is the only solution.

Dents
Small dents are usually easily cured by the 'Dentmaster' or equivalent process, which sucks or pushes out the dent (as long as the paint surface is still intact). Companies offering dent removal services usually come to your home: consult your telephone directory.

Traditional flaking metallic paintwork of older Fords.

Peeling lacquer.

Paint polished through to primer.

15 Problems due to lack of use

– just like their owners, Escorts need exercise!

Cars, like humans, are at their most efficient if they exercise regularly. A run of at least ten miles, once a week, is recommended for any Escort.

Seized components

Pistons in callipers, slave and master cylinders can seize.

The clutch may seize if the plate becomes stuck to the flywheel because of corrosion.

Handbrakes (parking brakes) can seize if the cables and linkages rust. Pistons can seize in the bores due to corrosion.

Fluids

Old, acidic oil can corrode bearings.

Uninhibited coolant can corrode internal waterways. Lack of antifreeze can cause core plugs to be pushed out, even cracks in the block or head. Silt settling and solidifying can cause overheating.

Brake fluid absorbs water from the atmosphere and should be renewed every two years. Old fluid with a high water content can cause corrosion and pistons/callipers to seize (freeze) and can cause brake failure when the water turns to vapour near hot braking components.

Even old petrol can deteriorate, resulting in poor running or failure to start.

Tyre problems

Tyres that have had the

Brakes can seize, but careful manipulation may free a sticking drum.

After a long stint of inactivity it's wise to renew brake fluid.

weight of the car on them in a single position for some time will develop flat spots, resulting in some (usually temporary) vibration. The tyre walls may have cracks or (blister-type) bulges, meaning new tyres are needed. No matter how authentic they look, be extra-cautious if attempting to drive an Escort on its original rubber!

Shock absorbers (dampers)

With lack of use, the dampers will lose their elasticity or even seize. Creaking, groaning and stiff suspension are signs of this

Tyres don't take kindly to being left standing.

problem – although some modified Escorts ride harshly and noisily anyway!

Rubber and plastic

Radiator hoses may have perished and split, possibly resulting in the loss of all coolant. Window and door seals can harden and leak. Gaiters/boots can crack. Wiper blades will harden.

Electrics

The battery will be of little use if it has not been charged for many months. Earthing/grounding problems are common when the connections have corroded. Old bullet- and spade-type electrical connectors commonly rust/corrode and will need disconnecting, cleaning and protection (eg Vaseline). Sparkplug electrodes will often have corroded in an unused engine. Wiring insulation can harden and fail.

Rotting exhaust system

Exhaust gas contains a high water content, so exhaust systems corrode very quickly from the inside when the car is not used.

16 The Community
– key people, organisations and companies in the Escort world

Old Escorts form a healthy chunk of the classic Ford scene, which brings together owners of everything from custom cars to factory-original concours machines.

All tastes are catered for, and each Escort has the backing of multiple owners' clubs, internet forums and dedicated spares specialists.

Although there's plenty of support for standard Escorts, it's fair to say lots of parts suppliers concentrate on modifications and motorsport conversions, for which there's a large crossover. That's in some way thanks to Escorts' ever-successful competition usage (no historic rally is complete without an old Escort), and also because buying go-faster goodies has always been integral with ownership of sporting Fords.

Despite the breadth of the Escort scene, few workshops are dedicated to run-of-the-mill repairs and renovation. The reason is quite simple – Escorts are essentially such basic machines that it's traditional for owners or local garages to tackle the work themselves. Even so, any Escort builder or performance specialist should be more than qualified to take care of general maintenance. Similarly, any firm that restores Escorts should be well placed to offer advice and inspections of a car you're intending to purchase.

The best way to find a suitable expert is to seek recommendations from other Escort enthusiasts. And the best way to find like-minded Escort fans is to join a relevant owners' club or internet forum. Most clubs will be able to put you in touch with decent specialists, and if they can't, their members certainly will.

Escort folk are generally a friendly bunch, providing guidance and banter in equal doses. You might even find a helpful local enthusiast willing to cast an expert eye over an Escort you're looking to buy.

Clubs and forums have countless other benefits too, including access to spare parts, insurance deals, shows, track days, nights out and holiday tours.

Clubs and forums

AVO Owners' Club
www.avoclub.com

1300E Owners' Club
www.1300eownersclub.org

Ford RS Owners' Club
PO Box 408
Grays
Essex
RM17 9ED
08702 406215
www.rsownersclub.co.uk

Ford RS Owners' Club of Australia
PO Box 2294
Greenhills
NSW 2323
www.rsownersclubaust.com.au

Ford RS Owners' Club Ireland
www.rsownersclubireland.ie

Sporting Escort Owners' Club
30 Rowan Way
Thurston
Bury St Edmunds
Suffolk
IP31 3PU
www.seoc.co.uk

Rallye Sport Escorts
bbs.rallyesportescorts.co.uk

Turbosport
www.turbosport.co.uk

RS2 Online
www.rs2.co.uk

Classic Ford forum (Australia)
www.classicford.mine.nu

RS Motorsport forum (Australia)
PO Box 1150
Springwood
QLD 4127
rsmotorsport.com.au

Specialists, parts and modifications
Andy Stapley Motorsport
07974 150380
www.mk1escorts.co.uk

Burton Power
020 8518 9136
www.burtonpower.com

Classictrim
01268 415166
www.classictrim.co.uk

East Kent Trim Supplies
01304 611681
www.classiccar-trim.com

The Escort Agency
01834 860 929
www.theescortagency.net

Escort-tec
www.escort-tec.co.uk

Gartrac Motorsport
01428 682263
www.gartrac.com

Mexico Mark
www.mexicomarks.co.uk

Old Ford Auto Services
01344 422731
www.oldfordautos.co.uk

Prepfab Motorsport Engineering
01427 858114
www.prepfab.co.uk

Rally Design
01227 792792
www.rallydesign.co.uk

Retro-Ford
01536 747978
www.retro-ford.co.uk

Useful sources of information
Classic Ford magazine
World-leading monthly magazine for classic Fords.

Retro Ford magazine
Monthly magazine for modified old Fords.

Factory-original Sporting Mk1 Escorts
By the author of this title, giving details and full-colour photographs of factory specifications, equipment and finishes of sporting Mk1 Escorts.

Factory-original Sporting Mk2 Escorts
By the author of this title, giving details and full-colour photographs of factory specifications, equipment and finishes of sporting Mk2 Escorts.

Ford Escort and Cortina Mk I and Mk II Restoration Manual
Kim Henson's dated but very useful practical manual covering stripdown, repair and renovation.

17 Vital statistics
– essential data at your fingertips

Technical specifications
Engine
1.1: 1097cc; four-cylinder; OHV; eight-valve; 42-48bhp; 50-54lbft
1.3: 1297cc; four-cylinder; OHV; eight-valve; 49-57bhp; 63-67lbft
1.3 GT/Sport/1300E: 1297cc; four-cylinder; OHV; eight-valve; 64-74bhp; 68-70lbft
1.6 Mexico/Sport/Ghia: 1599cc; four-cylinder; OHV; eight-valve; 83-86bhp; 92lbft
1.6 Twin Cam: 1558cc; four-cylinder; DOHC; eight-valve; 109.5bhp; 106.5lbft
1.6 RS1600: 1601cc; four-cylinder; DOHC; 16-valve; 120bhp; 112lbft
1.6 RS Mexico: 1593cc; four-cylinder; OHC; eight-valve; 93bhp; 92lbft
1.8 RS1800: 1834cc; four-cylinder; DOHC; 16-valve; 115bhp; 120lbft
2.0 RS2000: 1993cc; four-cylinder; OHC; eight-valve; 100-110bhp; 108-119lbft

Transmission
Four-speed manual or three-speed automatic, rear-wheel drive.

Suspension
Front
MacPherson struts with integral shock absorbers, coil springs and anti-roll bar (most models) or compression struts (pre-1969).

Rear
Semi-elliptic leaf springs, telescopic rear shock absorbers and anti-roll bar (most models) or radius rods (RS models).

Brakes
Front
8in drums, 8.6in discs (Mk1) or 9.625in discs (Mk2).

Rear
8-9in drums (depending on model). Larger-engined models with servo assistance.

Steering
Rack and pinion.

Wheels
3.5x12in, 4.5x12in, 5x13in or 5.4x13in steels (depending on model); 5.5x13-6x13in alloys (depending on model).

Dimensions
Mk1
Length: saloon 156.6in (3978mm); estate 160.8in (4084mm). Weight: 1641lb (744kg) to 2018lb (915kg).

Mk2
Length: saloon 156.6in (3978mm); RS2000 163.1in (4142mm); estate 160.8in (4084mm). Weight: 1844lb (838kg) to 2075lb (941kg).

Production figures
Mk1
2,228,349 (Europe) including …
  Twin Cam: 1263
  RS1600: 1154
  Mexico: 10,352
  RS2000: 5334

Mk2
1,808,395 (Europe) including …
  RS1800: 109
  RS Mexico: 2290
  RS2000: 25,638
  Harrier: 1500

Index